"Rev. Dr. Espinosa reinvigorates the Apostles' Creed by articulating how it is the perfect framework for Christians to use to defend their faith in the current cultural climate. It includes relevant encouragement on how to faithfully bear witness to the truths set before us in God's word, while also highlighting the importance of doing so with gentleness and respect. It is a must-read for those seeking a refreshing reminder that the foundations of our faith, God's word and the Apostles' Creed, are not only eternally true but also the best resource for addressing the complex problems that face the Christian today. Espinosa is a master of translating complex ideas into digestible and palatable language for our twenty-first-century minds. This book eloquently meets many great needs that we have in the church today!"

—AARON PULS, Instructor of Theology, Crean Lutheran High School, Irvine, California

"*Contending for Christ Through the Creed* is an invaluable resource for anyone teaching the catechism to any age group, as it uses the Apostles' Creed to address the pressing questions of our generation about the Christian faith. It also serves as a powerful tool for both learning and teaching evangelism, providing a gospel-centered framework that keeps conversations focused on the essential truths of Christianity. Rev. Dr. Espinosa's work is both insightful and thought-provoking, seamlessly weaving responses to common skeptical questions about God, Scripture, Jesus, salvation, and eternal life into the familiar structure of the Apostles' Creed. Additionally, it reassures lifelong Christians by demonstrating the reasonableness and truthfulness of the faith, equipping them to answer challenging questions with confidence."

—ROSS JOHNSON, Director, LCMS World Relief and Human Care Disaster Response

"When some would tell us that we have to pick up the weapons of our enemies if we want to win, Espinosa reminds us that our God is our hope; he is the powerful one, and we are the most effective when we ground our lives in his unchanging truth and love. Espinosa brings us 'back to the basics,' with a tour through our creeds, deeply rooted in Scripture, and accompanied by practical applications to contemporary cultural issues addressed from the heart of our deeply gracious God."

—RACHEL FERGUSON, Professor of Business, Concordia University Chicago

"During their arduous journey through the wilderness, disciples of Christ the world over have been led by the Holy Spirit throughout history to stand firm in the faith delivered to the saints. Along the way, they have often faced suspicion about or opposition to their claims. Exhorting Christians today to contend for the faith without being contentious, Dr. Espinosa unpacks what makes Christian claims suspect in North America today. Using the Apostles' Creed as his roadmap, the author responds to objections to the church's confession by offering a Gospel-centered, theologically winsome, and pastorally caring account of God's loving purposes for his creation through Jesus Christ. Through storytelling, biblical exposition, theological reflection, and practical questions for discussion in each chapter, Espinosa invites us to revel in and proclaim to others the beauty of living, moving, and having our being in our merciful triune God: Father, Son, and Holy Spirit."

—LEOPOLDO SANCHEZ, Professor of Theology, Concordia Seminary, St. Louis, Missouri

"Rev. Dr. Espinosa has done it again! A real triumph! This work will help you to find a way to communicate the truth of our faith in a winsome and faithful way. You will learn that speaking the creed is telling the story of our faith in a steadfast way. Rev. Dr. Espinosa has a delightful way of weaving story with truth that makes the journey enjoyable to the end."

—ROBERT SUNDQUIST, Pastor, Faith Community Lutheran Church and Schools, Las Vegas, Nevada

Contending for Christ
Through the Creed

Contending for Christ Through the Creed

Apologetics for Loving Answers on the Christian Faith

ALFONSO ESPINOSA

Foreword by Uwe Siemon-Netto

WIPF & STOCK · Eugene, Oregon

CONTENDING FOR CHRIST THROUGH THE CREED
Apologetics for Loving Answers on the Christian Faith

Copyright © 2025 Alfonso Espinosa. All rights reserved. Except for brief quotations in critical publications or reviews, no part of this book may be reproduced in any manner without prior written permission from the publisher. Write: Permissions, Wipf and Stock Publishers, 199 W. 8th Ave., Suite 3, Eugene, OR 97401.

Wipf & Stock
An Imprint of Wipf and Stock Publishers
199 W. 8th Ave., Suite 3
Eugene, OR 97401

www.wipfandstock.com

PAPERBACK ISBN: 979-8-3852-4446-1
HARDCOVER ISBN: 979-8-3852-4447-8
EBOOK ISBN: 979-8-3852-4448-5

05/27/25

Scripture quotations are from The ESV® Bible (The Holy Bible, English Standard Version®), © 2001 by Crossway, a publishing ministry of Good News Publishers. Used by permission. All rights reserved.

From *Luther's Works Volumes 1-30, 69* © 1958-2009 Concordia Publishing House. Used with permission. All rights reserved. cph.org.

From *Luther's Small Catechism* © 1958-2009 Concordia Publishing House. Used with permission. All rights reserved. cph.org.

From *Concordia Commentary: Luke* © 1958-2009 Concordia Publishing House. Used with permission. All rights reserved. cph.org.

From *Concordia: The Lutheran Confessions* © 1958-2009 Concordia Publishing House. Used with permission. All rights reserved. cph.org.

From *Concordia Commentary: Hebrews* © 1958-2009 Concordia Publishing House. Used with permission. All rights reserved. cph.org.

Excerpted from: *Charting the End Times* by Tim LaHaye and Thomas Ice, Copyright © 2001 Pre-Trib Research Center. Published by Harvest House Publishers, Eugene, Oregon 97408. www.harvesthousepublishers.com.

Quotations from *History, Law, and Christianity* by John Warwick Montgomery are used with permission from New Reformation Publications.

Material from *Reincarnation: The Missing Link in Christianity*, by Elizabeth Clare Prophet with Erin L. Prophet, reprinted by permission of Summit University Press.

Taken from *The Case for Faith: A Journalist Investigates the Toughest Objections to Christianity* by Lee Strobel, Copyright © 2000 used by permission of HarperCollins Christian Publishing. www.harpercollinschristian.com

Taken from *The Case for the Resurrected of Jesus* © Copyright 2004 by Gary R. Habermas and Michael R. Licona. Published by Kregel Publications, Grand Rapids, MI. Used by permission of the publisher. All rights reserved.

The Great Divorce by C. S. Lewis copyright © 1946 C. S. Lewis Pte. Ltd. Extract reprinted by permission.

Rev. Peter Bender,
my friend who contends for the faith in more ways than I can count,
and
my grandchildren since the last book, Greyson and Alethea.

Contents

Foreword: The Passing Cloudburst — ix
Preface — xiii
Acknowledgments — xv
Abbreviations — xvii
Introduction: Contending While Loving — 1

PART I | CONTENDING FOR THE FAITH ACCORDING TO THE FIRST ARTICLE OF THE CREED

1. Contending for Identity: "I" — 19
2. Culture and the Old "I" — 30
3. Contending for the Father — 41
4. Contending for the Creator — 52

PART II | CONTENDING FOR THE FAITH ACCORDING TO THE SECOND ARTICLE OF THE CREED

5. Contending for Jesus Christ of Real History — 69
6. Contending for Jesus, God Who Died — 88
7. Contending for Jesus, the Death of Death — 108
8. Contending for Jesus, the Keeper of Promises Coming Again — 124

CONTENTS

PART III | CONTENDING FOR THE FAITH ACCORDING TO THE THIRD ARTICLE OF THE CREED

9	Contending for the Holy Christian Church	141
10	Contending for Our Same Bodies Raised	153
11	Contending for the Life Everlasting	167

Conclusion	179
Bibliography	181
Topical & Names Index	185
Scriptural Index	191

Foreword

The Passing Cloudburst

I may be forgiven for modifying statements by two eminent theologians, one alive, the other long gone. The first is my pastor, Alfonso Espinosa, author of this admirable volume on the Apostles' Creed. In the preface he writes, "By all accounts US culture has long past moved from 'post-Christian . . .' to 'anti-Christian.'" This is true, but I should like to nuance it based on my observations in Germany.

As for Luther, he seems to provide an explanation for Espinosa's observation. Luther wrote, "For you should know that God's word and grace is like a passing shower of rain which does not return where it has once been."[1] In other words, the cloudburst will move on, drench another spot, and make it fruitful while the previous location dries up and becomes barren.

When I spent two months in hospital some time ago, a night nurse from Kenya looked after me. She told me that she returned to her country for two months every year to regale in the huge awakening back home, especially among the young people. The Christian faith is blossoming widely in many parts of Africa, including Ethiopia, Tanzania, and South Sudan. More remarkable still is the cloudburst drenching China, which by the middle of this century is expected to be home to more Christians than any other country in the world despite their persecution of Christians in this Communist nation; as Tertullian (AD 160–240) wrote, "The oftener we [Christians] are mown down by you, the more in number we grow; the blood of Christians is seed."[2]

1. Luther, *Christian in Society*, 352.
2. Tertullian, *Apology* 50 (ANF 3:55).

Foreword

Yet while the gospel has moved south and east geographically, it is also returning to the land it left,[3] though without affecting its original population, at least not for now, as we can observe in Germany where thousands of Persian migrants have converted to Christianity and thousands more are continuing to do so.

This isn't the place to tell the fascinating story of a much wider switch of Muslims to Christianity.[4] Suffice it to note what Rev. Dr. Christian Tiews, an LCMS missionary working among Iranians in Germany, once observed to me about them: "They are mainly upper middle-class and well-educated,"[5] which is to say, thinking people.

This is where Reverend Espinosa comes in with his commitment about apologetics, "the exercise of giving a reasonable answer for the hope that is within us." Point for point he provides reasonable answers to the questions raised by the crisp Apostles' Creed, "the Creed of creeds," he writes, quoting the Swiss-born theologian Philip Schaff (1819–1893).[6]

With his remark about a reasonable answer, Espinosa ventures into the tricky field of faith and reason. According to Luther, reason is a gift of God to mankind to find our way around this unredeemed world. Reason, he said, can inform us that there is a God but not about what God is like—namely, that he takes on human flesh, suffers, and dies for our sins, thus redeeming us. Only faith, a property of Christ's spiritual realm, which Luther calls the right-hand kingdom, can do this.[7] Reason, on the other hand, is an attribute of God's left-hand realm, which he rules in a hidden manner through us, his masks.[8]

---

3. Reverend Tiews, a German and American dual national and former geologist, learned Farsi in one year to preach and preside in divine services for Iranian and Afghan migrants in northern Germany.

4. Cf. Siemon-Netto, "Muslim Dreams."

5. Christian Tiews, in conversation with the author, Jan 15, 2008.

6. Schaff, *History of Creeds*, 14.

7. "Beyond [temporal government] there is yet a spiritual kingdom in which Christ rules in the hearts of men; this kingdom we cannot see, because it consists only in faith and will continue until the Last Day. These are two kingdoms: the temporal, which governs with the sword and is visible; and the spiritual, which governs solely with grace and with the forgiveness of sins." Luther, *Word and Sacrament*, 164. See also Luther, *Christian in Society*, 88, 91, 129.

8. "God could easily give you grain and fruit without your plowing and planting.... He could give children without using men and women. But He does not want to do this. Instead, He joins man and woman so that it appears to be the work of man and woman, and yet He does it under the cover of such masks. We have the saying: 'God gives every

Foreword

This poses a dilemma. Bright people from Persia bring the gospel back to apostate Germany, ostensibly at least in part because they grasp the gospel; apologetics provide "reasonable" answers to our hopes. We can go further: gone are the days when most members of the hard sciences found it necessary to coquet with their atheism. Today, the intelligent design movement, once denounced as pseudoscientific, is gaining ground especially among cosmologists but also biologists and physicians. They have come to conclude that the universe must have been created by an intelligent being, though they refrain from calling him God.

That still leaves us squarely in the left-hand kingdom, as does President Ronald Reagan's amusing remark: "I have long been unable to understand the atheist in this world of so much beauty. And I've had an unholy desire to invite some atheists to a dinner and then serve the most fabulous gourmet dinner that has ever been concocted and, after dinner, ask them if they believe there was a cook."[9]

So, what now? I posit that once one believes in God one can pray for faith bridging the two kingdoms. If God answers the prayer, then the new believer can cheerfully recite the Apostles' Creed.

Epiphany, 2025
UWE SIEMON-NETTO, PHD

---

good thing, but not just by waving a wand.' God gives all good gifts; but you must lend a hand and take the bull by the horns; that is, you must work and thus give God good cause and a mask." Luther, *Selected Psalms*, 114–15.

9. Reagan, "Remarks."

Preface

By all accounts US culture has long past moved from "post-Christian culture" to "anti-Christian culture." But this does not mean one iota that Christians should compromise the command of our Lord to love God and *then* to love our neighbor (Matt 22:37–39). And, of course, the commandments of Jesus must be kept in that order.[1]

In fact, more than ever, Christians must move away from defensive positions that present antagonism for those whose worldview permits the terrible confusion with which we are confronted in the culture. With greater understanding, it is for the church to "contend for the faith" (Jude 3) in such a way that unashamedly delivers the wisdom and light of God's word while making clear to whomever we speak that we know we, too, are sinners. We also contend that we are sinners committed to loving other sinners so that all would know the glorious freedom of the gospel from the bonds of sin, death, and the power of the devil.

I have had a longtime concern for maintaining a commitment to Christian apologetics in the church, but in such a way as to seek to learn how to present it with the life of Christ radiating through us Christians. Jesus never had to be argumentative. His "contending" for the faith had no need for being contentious. He was unafraid and full of commitment and sacrifice to serve whomever he interacted with.

Apologetics is the exercise of giving a reasonable answer for the hope that is within us (1 Pet 3:15). It is a subset of systematic theology which organizes all doctrine (teaching) of the Christian faith. It is—as I like to teach it—a scaffolding that serves the gospel.[2] Only the Holy Spirit working

---

1. If we reverse the order and love our neighbor *before* God, then the word of Christ will be compromised in the name of a misguided "love" that embraces the moral relativism of the culture.

2. I explain this view more thoroughly in my essay within *Theologia et Apologia*. See Espinosa, "Apologetics."

Preface

through the gospel of Jesus can change people. Apologetics simply supports the transmission of the gospel as it demonstrates that the gospel is of real history, understandable (even while presenting deep mysteries), and logical (even while correcting sinful reason). It does not "clear a path" for the gospel, but it serves the gospel for establishing common ground for communicating with different outlooks and worldviews.

This volume humbly asserts that culture should not be the framework in which Christians present the answers desperately needed by the world today. Rather, we should confidently employ the frameworks already handed down to us in the holy church. These frameworks are catechetical, and they are of the word of Christ.

The volume you are now reading is a first step for my vision for how to equip Christians to give an answer while they contend for the faith to free people in our culture from spiritual darkness and rationalistic confusion. In it, the Apostles' Creed is our guide. In writing the book, I was delighted to witness the flow of how the Lord has given us an approximately seventeen-hundred-year-old guide for addressing the tremendous needs of our world in the twenty-first century.

This is why this book has been written. It is for equipping you, the reader, to present the beautiful symmetry of the saving faith applied to real challenges confronting our culture today, with all the people for whom Jesus died, rose, and desires to save (1 Tim 2:4). And as these resources are presented for your witness to the truth and to serve people tangled in the Gordian knot of the world, may we with excitement share the bold stroke of the gospel leading to glorious freedom in Christ.

Let us now joyfully be led by the outline of the great creed of the church, the Apostles' Creed, so that our contending not be of our power and effort (which will always fail), but rather led by the Holy Spirit through the faith once delivered. This is *Contending for Christ Through the Creed*.

Acknowledgments

This current volume is something I was carrying with me in my mind for quite some time even before my trilogy on faith and culture. I am therefore sincerely grateful to Wipf and Stock Publishers for picking it up for publication. Interestingly enough, it was Wipf and Stock that first published a chapter I wrote in a book on Christian apologetics entitled *Theologia et Apologia: Essays in Reformation Theology and Its Defense Presented to Rod Rosenbladt*. In that volume, I had the honor of having the anchor essay entitled, "Apologetics as Pastoral Theology," which was published back in 2007 (a mere eighteen years ago).

Behind the scenes toward the final product of this current volume was Courtney Jorstad, who was extraordinary in either securing permissions or verifying public domains for all citations. In addition, Jon and Veronica Steele put me in the position for greater efficiency in my writing and research by setting up a new state-of-the-art workstation for me (one of the reasons I tell people I have such an incredible Christian congregation, as they are always taking care of me, their senior pastor).

Another one of my parishioners providing invaluable assistance was Julie Stiegmeyer, who provided a thorough editorial pass through my rough draft before final submission to the publisher for their last stage editing. Julie put me in the position to save a lot of time through her fine-tuning of the manuscript. Once in the hands of Wipf & Stock I had the privilege to work with copy editor Hannah Starr who was fabulous in providing topflight refinements.

In the process I had need to get away from it all for some peace and quiet to focus on the main writing portions. For this, Brian and Lareen Stone hosted me to hide away in their beautiful home, tucked away upstairs with my own dedicated facilities.

Acknowledgments

I would be remiss not to mention those who formed me to be able to elaborate upon Christian apologetics even at the popular level in this volume. During my undergraduate years at Concordia University Irvine, two men influenced me in the field—namely, Dr. Rod Rosenbladt and Dr. John Warwick Montgomery.

After being trained at a great seminary for pastoral ministry (MDiv), I served as a regular parish pastor for almost ten years when I realized that I could benefit from some graduate-level training in apologetics.

During this transition to Biola, Larry Martin—my father-in-law—was my patron enabling me to continue my apologetics training.

The faculty at Biola University, La Mirada, further equipped me with an MA program that honed my skills in the field. I am especially grateful to Dr. Craig Hazen, Dr. J. P. Moreland, Dr. William Lane Craig, Dr. John Bloom, Dr. Ron Rhodes, and other gifted faculty. Even my PhD studies in England were bolstered by this delightful master's program.

Along the way, my parish, Saint Paul's Lutheran Church of Irvine, has always been extraordinarily supportive of my writing and research. Not only do they grant me generous annual vacation time each year, but every seventh year comes with an additional sabbatical, a solid month, to delve into one of my favorite avocations in writing.

My last and certainly my most important supporter is my wife, Traci Dawn Espinosa, who encourages and sacrifices for me so that I may do what I love doing. I am blessed with the perfect counterpart who conducts her own apologetics towards me, helping me slow enough to smell life's roses along the way.

None of the above, however, could ever occur without Jesus, the author and finisher of our faith. To him be the glory for anyone this volume might benefit.

Epiphany, 2025
Rev. Alfonso Espinosa, PhD

Abbreviations

ANF	*Ante-Nicene Fathers*
BAGD	*Greek-English Lexicon of the New Testament and Other Early Christian Literature* (Bauer-Arndt-Gingrich-Danker)
NPNF[1]	*Nicene and Post-Nicene Fathers*, Series 1
NPNF[2]	*Nicene and Post-Nicene Fathers*, Series 2
v.	verse

Introduction: Contending While Loving

CONTEND WITHOUT BEING CONTENTIOUS

In the little single-chapter book of Jude, we find this jewel: "Beloved, although I was very eager to write to you about our common salvation, I found it necessary to write appealing to you to contend for the faith that was once for all delivered to the saints" (v. 3).

To *contend* here does not mean to be mean-spirited. It does not mean to lower oneself to the ways of the world and the sinful flesh. We hear the colloquialism "bone of contention," which has the negative connotation of a debate or argument. Fair enough, but for the *Christian* enterprise, we cannot lose the greater context of Holy Scripture.

First Peter 3:15 presents the Christian as giving an answer—testimony—"in gentleness and respect." There is no slinking into reasons to indulge the flesh to insult someone who does not agree with us. Even toward, and perhaps especially toward, someone who disagrees with us, we are called to be gentle towards that person, and to recall the other party always present, the Lord Jesus Christ. Because of his holy presence, all things must be conducted with respect. The King is there, and we have the privilege to honor him, not by giving into anger but in maintaining self-control and a demeanor worthy of the gospel.

That is, we Christians ought to argue without being argumentative, testify to the truth without the need to win an argument, give an answer without becoming defensive, and contend while we avoid returning evil for evil.[1]

---

1. See Rom 12:21.

Introduction: Contending While Loving

The thrust of Jude's message presents the Holy Spirit appealing to us to contend for the faith so that regardless of the cultural circumstances, nothing of the faith is compromised. To contend in this sense is to hold to truth, the whole truth, and nothing but the truth of God's holy word. Christians do not compromise nor cease doing what God has called the holy church to always do: believe in, hold fast to, worship in accord with, and witness to the faith once delivered, and none other.[2]

It is true that in the following verse of Jude, certain people were trying to "pervert the grace of God into sensuality and deny our only Master and Lord, Jesus Christ" (v. 4). Thus, there were negative circumstances confronting the early church receiving Jude's instruction.

This may mean that while we are contending, we will often feel the hostility of what the world presents to us and everyone else. The Scriptures do not deny this reality. Saint Paul wrote, "For we do not wrestle against flesh and blood, but against the rulers, against the authorities, against the cosmic powers over this present darkness, against the spiritual forces of evil in the heavenly places" (Eph 6:12). There are always spiritual forces at work and the ones against Jesus Christ will put us in situations in which we must hold on with tenacity and be unafraid to speak the faith once delivered in broad daylight.

Luther elaborated upon Jude 3–4:

> Wicked men will come, and they will not persevere. They always have this fault of teaching something different and new. A wicked spirit, not rooted in solid doctrine, causes this. The flesh becomes sluggish; it sees to it that we forget the word and grow tired of it. The bishop [pastor] should not worry that he is often teaching the same thing. . . . [Paul] opposes diseases of doctrine; that is, doctrine should be right, stable, and constant. . . . Those who do not have a doctrine that is sure and constant do not teach.[3]

Not surprisingly, Saint Paul's teaching is complementary to Saint Jude's teaching. Saint Paul wrote, "Only let your manner of life be worthy of the gospel of Christ, so that whether I come and see you or am absent, I may hear of you that you are standing firm in one spirit, with one mind striving side by side for the faith of the gospel" (Phil 1:27).

---

2. Christians hold to the objective faith—teaching and revelation of God's holy word—while having in their hearts saving subjective faith, through which they believe in and trust in the Lord Jesus and his word. Here we are referring to the objective faith.

3. Luther, *Titus, Philemon, and Hebrews*, 32.

Introduction: Contending While Loving

Thankfully, our contending, standing firm, and striving is not in isolation, working as if we were lone rangers. We are rather "we" indeed, together as the body of Christ. Individual Christians are not individual as we might be apt to believe, but members of the temple of God, the holy church.

As Christians standing together, we are instructed by Saint Paul to be conscientious and watchful about our way of life which is designed to keep us ready—precisely—to stand firm in one spirit, and with one mind striving (a wonderful synonym for *contending*) for the faith of the gospel. The Holy Spirit instructs that in the face of possible temptation, Christians should be unafraid (Phil 1:28) while facing the reality that we are also permitted to suffer for the sake of Christ while engaged in conflict (Phil 1:29–30). This is not a curse but a great honor, even if only seen through the eyes of faith.

The world, sin, and the devil are eager to translate any conflict into animosity and hatred, even within the soul of the Christian. But this cannot be for the baptized children of God. Rather, Christians emulate their Savior, who did not give in to fear or unnecessary words even while standing in front of Pilate before being sentenced to be crucified.

That is, our contending for the faith is to be consistent with the instruction of Christ: "But I say to you, love your enemies and pray for those who persecute you, so that you may be sons of your Father who is in heaven. For he makes his sun rise on the evil and on the good, and sends rain on the just and on the unjust" (Matt 5:44–45).

CONTEND FOR THE FAITH ONCE DELIVERED

The faith once delivered, otherwise known as objective faith, is not the same as the saving faith in the heart which God creates by the power of the Holy Spirit working through the word and sacraments of the Lord Jesus Christ.[4] This faith is created in us by God to be like a spiritual organ (analogous to a physical organ like the heart muscle). The word of Christ is clear as to

---

4. *Fides quae* is the objective faith / teaching that has been handed down to us through the centuries by the church holding to the truth of the word of God. Here, think of faith as in the image of a statue of Luther holding to the Holy Scriptures. Luther took his stand on the word of God / THE faith of God, the teaching of God, the revelation of God, the truth, and our foundation. *Fides qua* is the faith in us that believes and trusts in the gospel of Jesus Christ. The first form of faith is objective and outside of us; the second form is subjective and describes the faith in our hearts that holds to Jesus. Think of Rom 1:17: "From faith for faith." *From* objective faith of God's holy word for the creating—by the Holy Spirit—of the faith in our hearts to hold to Jesus alone *for* our life and salvation.

Introduction: Contending While Loving

how we receive this subjective faith in us: "So faith comes from hearing, and hearing through the word of Christ" (Rom 10:17). It also comes in and through Holy Baptism: "And now why do you wait? Rise and be baptized and wash away your sins, calling on his name" (Acts 22:16). The faith Holy Baptism demands is the faith Holy Baptism grants by the power of the Holy Spirit, since the water prescribed by God contains the word of God which makes it a saving water through faith.[5]

Here in Saint Jude's letter, however, Christians are being admonished to contend for THE faith, the objective teaching: God's word itself. It is the foundation of the entire body of Christ, and the gospel of Jesus Christ therein is the rock upon which Christ builds his church (Matt 16:18).

As a pastor for over three decades, I have received countless questions that start off as something like this: "What do you think about _____, pastor?" Or "Do you do believe that _____ is true?" There are, of course, many variations of this same question. And while my own personal trust in the heart and my faith in Jesus Christ is indispensable to and for me, I do not need my subjective faith to answer most of these questions. In fact, I have often replied to people, "It doesn't matter what I think or believe. All that matters is what the word of God says." This is our objective teaching and foundation. There are no "survey says" answers here. This is not about polling or wetting your finger to put in the air to check which direction the cultural wind is blowing so that you may accommodate your answer to please people and/or the culture.

The answer is never about the goal for pleasing people. The answer is *always* about the goal of being faithful to his word delivered / handed down to his church for all people.

These things have immense implications for "faith that contends." Streaming from our subjective faith is the conviction that we must be true to God—Father, Son, and Holy Spirit—to stand fast as we hold onto the objective faith of God's holy word without wavering. In our culture today, many things seem to have been sucked into the black hole of relativistic thinking from morals to beliefs, but there is one thing resistant to this gravitational pull: "The faith that was once for all delivered to the saints" (Jude 3).

God does not change: "For I the Lord do not change" (Mal 3:6). God's word does not change: "But the word of the Lord remains forever" (1 Pet

---

5. Titus 3:5: "He saved us, not because of works done by us in righteousness, but according to his own mercy, by the washing of regeneration and renewal of the Holy Spirit."

Introduction: Contending While Loving

1:25). We who are alive in Christ and hold fast to his word cannot cease / never change from contending for the faith of Christ. This is another unchanging feature of the sacred faith: *Christians must always contend for the faith, come rain or shine.*

CONTENDING: NOT JUST WHAT WE SAY, BUT HOW WE SAY IT

While avoiding contentiousness and at the same time being faithful to contend for the faith, we should also take into consideration the *way* in which we speak the truth in a culture that is quickly evolving from a post-Christian culture to, in many regions, an anti-Christian culture.

It is easy once groups are identified for people to slide into tribalism for the sake of distinguishing the good guys from the bad guys. This I found to be a characteristic surrounding teaching on the last things and end times.[6] Those who mishandle apocalyptic genre (as we encounter in the book of Revelation) anticipate a future end-time cosmic battle between the children of light and the children of darkness. The opposing side, of course, is always demonized. Christians who accept this sort of thinking bring the future end-time conflict into the present while stoking reasons to withhold love and concern for their neighbor.

When the world sees this inconsistency—even if they cannot put it into words—it is a small wonder why so many people are turned off by Christians. There are, of course, many who use perceived hypocrisy as an excuse to avoid the Christian church, but in other instances, hypocrisy may be true.

Whenever I conduct pre-engagement, engagement, or marital pastoral counseling, I often spend time on communication between the couple. We spend time considering basic facets:

1. The actual words we use
2. The *way* in which we speak those words (intonation, sincerity, consideration, etc.)
3. The body language and gestures which accompany words and style (e.g., it isn't a good idea to have your arms crossed while saying, "I love you")

---

6. Espinosa, "Apocalyptic Anxiety."

Introduction: Contending While Loving

4. The practice of active listening while intentionally taking in what the other person says: "I love you and want to understand what you are saying so that I can love you better"

When one blurts out a reaction without listening, this is not love but self-centeredness. The same basic principles apply to our contending for the faith. There is a *way* to communicate. There is a *how* to communicate, and we have the best Teacher to emulate. It is a method which goes against the grain of the world's animosity and knee-jerk condemnation.

COMMUNICATE LIKE JESUS

God woos. God declares. God comforts. God invites. God teaches. God calls. God hears. God listens. His communication covers a broad spectrum. When his people had lost their home and were living in exile, the Lord said through the prophet Isaiah, "Comfort, comfort my people, says our God. Speak tenderly to Jerusalem, and cry to her that her warfare is ended, that her iniquity is pardoned, that she has received from the Lord's hand double for all her sins" (Isa 40:1–2).

The Lord God was encouraging the prophet Elijah when he falsely believed he was the only prophet left standing. God instructed Elijah, "Go out and stand on the mount before the Lord" (1 Kgs 19:11). The Lord sent a mighty wind to tear the mountains, but the Lord was not in the wind; then he sent an earthquake, but the Lord was not in the earthquake; and then he sent a fire, but the Lord was not in the fire. "And after the fire the sound of a low whisper" (1 Kgs 19:12). God was at that point finally speaking to the discouraged prophet, but it was not a voice to frighten him but a voice to comfort him in a low whisper.

Try to imagine the sound of Jesus' voice. His was the voice that created all things. He spoke the universe into existence. "And God said, 'Let there be light,' and there was light" (Gen 1:3). The speaking God who creates is Jesus, God Almighty, the Word of God who *is* God (John 1:1–3). Jesus' speaking power is without limitation.

When he speaks, his words express the exuding authority of God. But we should not confuse his voice with a voice of one who needs to prove himself. He does not assert his power for his ego, to threaten us to get our

Introduction: Contending While Loving

acts together or else![7] He speaks rather to use his power to save us poor sinners in mercy.

Saint Peter experienced the restoring and healing words of Jesus. After Saint Peter had been fishing all night to no avail, Jesus said to him, "Put out into the deep and let down your nets for a catch." Saint Peter was incredulous, but he obeyed. The Scriptures record, "And when they had done this, they enclosed a large number of fish, and their nets were breaking" (Luke 5:4–6). How did Saint Peter respond to Jesus who spoke with such power and authority? The word records that Saint Peter fell overwhelmed by his sinful doubt at the knees of Jesus saying, "Depart from me, for I am a sinful man, O Lord" (Luke 5:8).

And yet Jesus did not punish him for his lack of faith but instead called Saint Peter to follow him. Jesus loves the doubters, the weak, the lost, and the sinners. His voice and his words must have surely conveyed the deepest love the world has ever known.

Having all power and authority does not translate into Jesus exerting his voice to frighten us, but he speaks tenderly to convey what he does with his almighty power: he uses it to rescue us from sin, death, and the power of the devil.

Jesus continues to speak to us in this tone: "Come to me, all who labor and are heavy laden, and I will give you rest" (Matt 11:28). To Nicodemus who needed guidance, Jesus challenged him, "Are you the teacher of Israel and yet you do not understand these things?" (John 3:10). But this was not to shut down the conversation. Jesus had garnered the Pharisee's full attention and went on to speak the gospel into Nicodemus's ears, heart, and mind. Nicodemus most likely became Jesus' disciple that very night.[8]

The rich young ruler who did not believe in Christ, though he persisted in his delusional[9] and yet sincere belief that he had kept the law of

---

7. But does not the Lord threaten sinners in Holy Scripture? He does, but the threats themselves bring no one to saving faith. On the other hand, they reveal the hard-heartedness of sinners who rebel against the Living God.

8. The Scriptures do not state that Nicodemus was converted on this occasion recorded in John 3, but this much we know: that Christ's word is a true means of grace which creates faith; furthermore, that Nicodemus essentially defended Christ in John 7:51; and more importantly, Nicodemus conducted himself as a true disciple of Christ while assisting Joseph of Arimathea in reverently preparing the Lord's body for burial after his crucifixion. In other words, Nicodemus had come to saving faith. He had heard the gospel, the same one we know so well as recorded in John 3:16: "For God so loved the world, that he gave his only Son, that whoever believes in him should not perish but have eternal life."

9. "Delusional" because it is impossible for sinners to keep God's law in the way

Introduction: Contending While Loving

God, also experienced Jesus' tender words. The text reads, "Jesus, looking at him, loved him, and said to him, 'You lack one thing: go, sell all that you have and give to the poor, and you will have treasure in heaven; and come, follow me'" (Mark 10:21).

Towards those who desired to execute the woman caught in adultery, Jesus announced no accusations against them but simply stood up from writing on the ground and said, "Let him who is without sin among you be the first to throw a stone at her" (John 8:7).

Even to Judas who was going to betray him, Jesus said without malice to him, "What you are going to do, do quickly" (John 13:27). To the officer who struck him in the presence of the high priest, Jesus only stated and asked, "If what I said is wrong, bear witness about the wrong; but if what I said is right, why do you strike me?" (John 18:23). This simple statement and question were probably designed to help the officer's soul.

When Pilate pushed for more insight from his interrogation of Christ, Jesus only reminded Pilate that the authority he would exert was directly from God. In other words, not only did Jesus not need to defend himself, but he taught Pilate that he had granted Pilate power to do what he was going to do.

These scenes from the New Testament are the fulfillment of what Isaiah wrote: "Like a lamb is led to the slaughter, and like a sheep that before its shearers is silent, so he opened not his mouth" (Isa 53:7b). He absolutely refused to open his mouth to speak evil against his persecutors. It just never happened. As a matter a fact, from the cross he prayed for those crucifying him and mocking him: "Father, forgive them, for they know not what they do" (Luke 23:34).

What might be considered among the most blatant seeming exceptions are the expulsions of the sellers in the temple (John 2:13-17 and Mark 11:15-17) and Jesus giving his diagnostic of the religious leaders as having the devil as their father (John 8:44). The first was done in honor of the Father, and the latter to convict for the sake of repentance.

For these same children of Israel, Jesus mourned: "O Jerusalem, Jerusalem, the city that kills the prophets and stones those who are sent to it! How often would I have gathered your children together as a hen gathers her brood under her wings, and you were not willing" (Matt 23:37).

---

which God demands: "For all have sinned and fall short of the glory of God" (Rom 3:23); "For whoever keeps the whole law but fails in one point has become guilty of all of it" (Jas 2:10).

Introduction: Contending While Loving

Why this overview on the way Jesus spoke (or did not speak)? Because it contextualizes and teaches how *we* ought to speak. The word *apologia* in 1 Pet 3:15 means "to make a defense."[10] But in what way? In what tone? The answer is in emulation of Jesus. Again, this is why Saint Peter was sure to qualify the answer, defense, or testimony: "Yet do it with gentleness and respect."

THE GAMUT OF COMMUNICATION FOR CONTENDING

Precisely because what we are describing here is *not* the way of the world, the glaring contrast in communication styles itself is a witness to the world that Christians really *are* different (unless the Christian is either ignorant or recalcitrant).

The variety of communication processes and approaches is fascinating in God's word. In Acts 17:2–3, three English words stand out (in the ESV translation) as to how Saint Paul was contending for the faith: "reasoned," "explaining," and "proving." The key word here in this section from the original Greek is *dialegomai*. The word means to discuss or conduct a discussion, which may include that which pertains to lectures which were likely to end in disputations.[11]

We gain a little more insight, however, as the scene shifts from Thessalonica, in the verses just mentioned, to Saint Paul's approach in Athens. At the Areopagus, we get vivid details of Saint Paul's method. His opening words tell the story of what kind of discussing and proving Saint Paul conducted: "Men of Athens, I perceive that in every way you are very religious" (Acts 17:22). Saint Paul did not insult the Athenians, nor was he being manipulative or deceitful. He was rather bringing out the significant common ground both he and the Athenians shared: they were very religious in the sense of having a hunger for truth.[12]

In other words, though Saint Paul and the Athenians were, in one sense, worlds apart, Saint Paul loved them. He was conducting himself in the image of Jesus, who did not come for some people but for all.

---

10. BAGD 96.

11. BAGD 185.

12. See my elaboration of this scene in Espinosa, *Faith That Engages*, ch. 6 ("Engagement's Example").

Introduction: Contending While Loving

THE NEED TO UNDERSTAND THE CULTURE

It is necessary to understand what the word of God means by urging Christians to contend for the faith once delivered, but unless the Christian church has its finger on the pulse of the culture, contending won't go very far. Aware of this "both/and" reality, Saint Paul described his missionary strategy: "I have become all things to all people, that by all means I might save some" (1 Cor 9:22b).[13]

And the only way *that* is going to happen is to make a real investment to know to whom we are speaking. Moreover, it is impossible to really know people without having a sense of the place in which they live, the traditions they follow, and the values they hold. To understand the culture is to have insight into the worldview of the people who live in that culture.

Understanding culture is not an easy task. One reason is the rate of cultural change. Another is that the influence of the church is becoming increasingly less impactful, if for no other reason than because Christian churches are closing at an alarming rate and major Christian denominations are declining.[14] And while it remains to be seen how the exponential growth of artificial intelligence (AI) and biotechnology will continue to impact the world, there is little doubt that changes will be significant.

At the very least, the ongoing surge of AI will increase the sense of human capability and power. The movement toward escalating personal autonomy will make it easier for people to believe that all they need is at their fingertips.

The most serious problem will be losing sight of the inestimable value of living incarnationally toward one another, face-to-face, live, and in living color, where one is there to catch the other if they fall. And the fact that a robot could do the catching is entirely beside the point.

How will we contend for the faith when faith is increasingly untethered from the church, or even worse, is perceived as insignificant (or even dangerous) and worthy of cancellation?

And yet even in the face of these serious questions, recall Solomon's words again: "There is nothing new under the sun" (Eccl 1:9). The human heart does not change, even if human bodies interface more with technology. The needs of the psyche and spirit will not change because people must

---

13. See my elaboration of this missionary strategy in Espinosa, *Faith That Engages*, ch. 5 ("Engagement's Attitude").

14. Something that is true across the board for all the major Christian church bodies, including non-Christian bodies.

still cope with loneliness, despair, and the need to love and to be loved; and most importantly, God will not change at all through the changes and chances of life. The Apostles' Creed outlines the faith once delivered—and unchanging—to the saints.

THE CREED INFORMS THE CULTURE

The holy church which contends for the faith can also interpret the culture through the lens of the faith. The faith itself is the diagnostic for the world no matter the time or place. The faith itself is our guide to the human heart and mind, and the deepest needs of the human soul "trans-time." Why are these things true? Because the faith communicates the word and the will of God, who knows his creation and its problems since the fall perfectly.

For this reason, this volume relies on the faith itself to provide a grid for seeing how to contend for the faith in our current place and time. This structure of the faith is found in what is the most popular creed in all of Christendom: the Apostles' Creed. This creed was not written by the first-century apostles, but it is an exquisite summary of what the apostles taught by the command of the Lord Jesus Christ. Schaff states, "As the Lord's Prayer is the Prayer of prayers, the Decalogue the Law of laws, so the Apostles' Creed is the Creed of creeds."[15]

As for the complaint against the creed by some Christians who assert that it is not found in the Holy Bible, this is tantamount to saying that the term "Holy Trinity" is not found in the Holy Bible. The point in both cases is that the *teaching* for these is found embedded in the Holy Scriptures. The creed provides sublime handles for the faith once delivered.

The First Article

Creation

> I believe in God, the Father Almighty, Maker of heaven and earth.

---

15. Schaff, *History of Creeds*, 14.

Introduction: Contending While Loving

The Second Article

Redemption

> And in Jesus Christ, his only Son, our Lord, who was conceived by the Holy Spirit, born of the Virgin Mary; suffered under Pontius Pilate, was crucified, died, and was buried. He descended into hell. The third day he rose again from the dead. He ascended into heaven and sits at the right hand of God, the Father Almighty. From thence he will come to judge the living and the dead.

The Third Article

Sanctification

> I believe in the Holy Spirit, the holy Christian church, the communion of saints, the forgiveness of sins, the resurrection of the body, and the life everlasting. Amen.

Every article of the creed is a direct summary of biblical teaching. Among those statements, what might be causing the most challenges for some include, "He descended into hell" in the second article; "rose again from the dead," also in the second article; and "the communion of saints" in the third article.

"He descended into hell" is of course the summary for 1 Pet 3:18–20:

> For Christ also suffered once for sins, the righteous for the unrighteous, that he might bring us to God, being put to death in the flesh but made alive in the spirit, in which he went and proclaimed to the spirits in prison, because they formerly did not obey, when God's patience waited in the days of Noah, while the ark was being prepared, in which a few, that is, eight persons, were brought safely through water.

God's word teaches clearly that after his death Jesus went to preach to the "spirits in prison." The Apostles' Creed includes this significant christological detail. It was after the inclusion of the descent that the final text of the creed was finalized, "no earlier than [AD] 370," and "the descent into

Introduction: Contending While Loving

hell then assumed... the triumph celebrated by Christ over the devil and his legions."[16]

"Rose again from the dead" challenges some because of its use of the word "again." Didn't Jesus rise from death *once*? Of course. The wording does not imply he rose twice, but that he was living bodily on the earth during two distinct time frames: the first time before his death, and the second time after he died and rose from death. In other words, the creed teaches that Christ was alive again after dying.

The "communion of saints" causes some dissonance in respect to the word "saints." Without belaboring the evolution of the word in some traditions, let us simply go to what the Holy Scriptures say. Christians are referred to in different ways in God's word. One way is through the literal Greek word for "saints" or "holy ones." For example, Saint Paul referred to *all* the Christians living in Ephesus as "saints / holy ones" in his greeting to the Ephesians (1:1). Why are Christians saints or holy ones? They are so on account of Jesus' righteousness and holiness imputed to them by God's grace through faith in the Savior. Christians are holy because they are *in Christ*, as Saint Paul describes about two hundred times in the New Testament.

But there is another word in this last example that might confuse some contemporary Christians. It is the word *communion*. It is, of course, a beautiful word that refers to the mystical union of all believers with the Lord Jesus Christ. To be in communion with Christ is to be one with Christ, united to him. And if all Christians are one with Christ, then they are also all one/united with one another. Thus, Christians are members of the body of Christ and comprise together the family of God. To be in communion with Jesus is to be in communion with all other Christians who are called "holy ones" or saints. Furthermore, this communion exists not only with the saints—Christians on earth—but also with those in heaven. Thus, Christians confess "the communion of saints" and may (and should) refer to one another as "brothers" or "sisters" in Christ.

There is perhaps another statement that stands out. Of all people to be named in the creed besides Jesus and his mother, Mary, why on earth do Christians keep repeating "Pontius Pilate"? That is a question—a quite important one at that—we will answer later in the book.

Because the creed is such a vital component of the faith once delivered, we will not consult the culture as to what questions should be answered, but

---

16. Pelikan, *Emergence*, 150–51.

we will consult the faith once delivered from God to the Christian church. This will inform us what the culture *needs* to hear and know. In this way, not only are Christians equipped to rightly contend for the faith in the culture, but the people in the culture stand to have what is most important presented to them for their lives to know the blessings of God. The outline of the creed accomplishes this.

Part 1 is, therefore, based on the first article of the creed. The first two chapters will consider the "I" of the believer who confesses it and how this new identity presents the answer to the "off-ness" all people sense about life (chapters 1 and 2). Chapter 3 is about how God may be found and come to be known as Father. Chapter 4 is on how to contend that he is indeed the Creator of all things by learning the evidence that he has placed upon and within creation.

Part 2 is on the second article of the creed. The next four chapters of this book focus on Jesus Christ. Chapter 5 is on the Christ of real history, the incarnate Christ. Chapter 6 contends for the God who died that we might know true religion over the trap of natural religion. Chapter 7 focuses on Christ as the death of death and how real history speaks to his resurrection. Finally, chapter 8 presents how Christians contend for the blessed hope of Christ's glorious second coming.

Part 3 with the final three chapters focuses on the third article of the creed. Chapter 9 is for the proper contending of the Holy Spirit as God whose greatest gifts to the church are the marks of the church so that we know where to connect to God. Chapter 10 contends for the real and physical resurrection of the body, and chapter 11 is on contending for the real heaven, the real hell, and God's unfathomable love for all people. Let us now launch into *Contending for Christ Through the Creed*.

INTRODUCTION DISCUSSION GUIDE: CONTENDING WHILE LOVING

UNCOVER INFORMATION

1. What does Jude 3 mean by "contend" for the faith?
2. What does Jude 3 mean by "the faith once delivered"? What "faith" is that?
3. How would you explain the difference between objective and subjective faith?

Introduction: Contending While Loving

4. How did Jesus our Lord communicate?
5. Why is the Apostles' Creed a good lens or framework for knowing what our culture needs?

DISCOVER MEANING

1. How do 1 Pet 3:15 and Phil 1:27 help us better understand contending for the faith?
2. What can be misleading when people ask us, "What do you believe about _____?" or "How do you feel about _____?"
3. Why are the basic components of communication important for contending for the faith?
4. Why is it important to understand the culture to contend for the faith more effectively?
5. What do some of the more confusing parts of the Apostles' Creed mean (e.g., Christ's descent, that he "rose again," and the "communion of saints")?

EXPLORE IMPLICATIONS

1. How do we contend without being contentious? How can we argue without being argumentative?
2. Why is it important to remind ourselves that our goal is not to "win" arguments?
3. What is the problem with demonizing opponents to the Christian faith while developing an "us" versus "them" mentality?
4. Why is understanding the culture important for contending for the faith?
5. Why is it important that the word of God inform the culture, instead of the culture informing Christians about life?

PART I

Contending for the Faith According to the First Article of the Creed

1

Contending for Identity: "I"

"I believe . . ."

WHAT ALL PEOPLE KNOW TO BE TRUE

In the movie series called *The Matrix*, we encounter traces of Eastern religious motifs which posit that the world we live in is illusory. In the case of the movie series, advanced machines had subdued humanity, putting them into a hibernation state to extract energy from their bodies. While existing as human batteries for the machines, the people themselves lived out a perpetual dream state that existed in an artificial cyber world called—you guessed it—the Matrix.[1]

While the dream world seemed as real as real could be, the main character just can't get away from his gut instinct that there is something wrong with his existence. All the world seems *off*; life is not as it ought to be. The story is about his discovery of this artificial dream world and his breaking out of it to discover his true self and liberation from the machines.

The flick makes for a good occasion for some popcorn and cinematic escapism, but as for the notion that people live with a basic awareness that something is wrong, the movie on this point is spot on even if its explanation is inaccurate.

The Apostles' Creed starts off with the confession: "*I* believe in . . ." The very first word is easy to take for granted, but we shouldn't because it is

1. Wachowski and Wachowski, *Matrix*.

referring to our life and identity—who and what we are—the moment the word "I" comes out of our mouths.

To understand the "I" according to the word of God informs us that until people grasp a biblical understanding of who we are, then what continues to grate on the conscience is that life is quite simply not as it ought to be. The "I" also explains why, until a person knows their Maker and his antidote to what is wrong with humanity, one can expect an ongoing soulish dissonance. Being separated from God generates the intuition that something is wrong with the world. This does not keep people from trying to solve the dilemma, but even our best efforts fail to make things better while demonstrating that whatever is wrong with life continues to hurt our bodies, minds, and souls.

At the same time, what is wrong does not seem external, but our consciences witness that the problem is something within us. Our problem is not a malevolent external wizard hiding behind a curtain pulling levers and turning knobs to orchestrate our lives, but rather is *internal*. And before anyone starts to conjure up images of aliens living inside our bodies, let's stick to reality and learn from the word of God.

The word of Christ informs us that our internal "I," before arriving to the "I" of the Apostles' Creed, has a problem. And to know this one thing is not only to understand the havoc that this disparity can cause in our lives, but this realization leads us to what God does about our "I" in such a way as to revitalize it and do something about that "not right" sense we carry around.

WHERE OUR "I" HAS BEEN

The word of God, the Holy Bible, is God's revelation and communication to all humanity about the most important things we should know about life. God's word is the basis for knowledge (like logic) and wisdom (like morality). It confirms important fundamentals of what all people know—in a limited way—because God has made these things universally known.[2]

---

2. All people apart from saving faith in Jesus Christ have the natural knowledge of God through the natural revelation, like the creation itself (Rom 1), and the imbedded conscience God has given to all humanity (Rom 2). For these two reasons alone, people, regardless of how they self-identify, are connected to their Creator and God. This natural knowledge, while vitally important, is not enough for a person to receive saving faith or to be born again / from above (John 3:3–8). These things will be elaborated upon in the section below on God the Father.

Contending for Identity: "I"

And one of the things all people know is that there is something wrong within themselves. The conscience knows not because religion is the "opiate of the masses" (vis-á-vis Marx), but because we possess—without anyone informing us—an awareness that some things are right and other things are wrong. And the result of this knowledge convicts us (unless we are trying hard to live in a state of denial) that we have not always done the right but have often chosen the wrong.

For example, no one needs a church background or to have read the Holy Bible to know

- it is wrong to betray a friend,
- it is wrong to harm someone in their body,
- it is wrong to take what is not your own.

Certainly, many people do these things all the time, but the point here is that when they do—even if they seek to repress their internal awareness—they know deep in their soul that this is not the way things ought to be, regardless of the rationalizations used to justify themselves.[3]

By violating what they know is right and true, people come to know shame, that there is something wrong with who and what they *are*. If their conscience is in good working order, individuals encounter guilt, that there is something wrong with their thoughts, words, and/or actions by way of commission or omission.

How did our respective "I's" get to this place? The Scriptures tell us. But first we must begin with the fact that humanity was created in the image of God.[4] "So God created man in his own image, in the image of God he created him; male and female he created them" (Gen 1:27). In this state of being, shame and guilt were nonexistent. Sin, which is lawlessness and rebellion against God, did not exist.

What is more, God who is love (1 John 4:8, 16) created his people to be able to love him. Our first parents, therefore, had the ability to *choose* to

---

3. Someone may assert the exception of a sociopath, to which I will not try to argue with as I am not a psychiatrist nor psychologist, though I would maintain that no one is beyond the reach of the Holy Spirit for help and healing.

4. The *imago Dei* is original righteousness when humanity was in perfect alignment with God's righteousness. That is, the mind and heart of God was indelibly marked within the mind and heart of Adam and Eve. If God had said, "Jump!" Adam and Eve would have asked, "How high?!" What God wanted, they wanted.

love God, and to have the ability to choose inherently means that people also have the ability not to choose, or to deny.

Saint Augustine characterized the first of four stages of humanity before sin came into the world as people having the condition of being "able to sin" and "able not to sin."[5] Being in this condition, people had the genuine capacity to love one another, especially God. For that love to be love, *there is no forcing the situation, no arm-twisting, and no preprogramming.* An AI-powered robot might look human and be programmed to express loving words and behaviors to their human purchasers, but everyone will know that this is a far cry from the real deal.

The bottom line here is that when our first parents chose to *not* love God, then love—pure love—itself became lost. People entered the second stage of humanity: not being able not to sin.[6]

OUR MESSED-UP "I"

It is impossible to describe the devastating effects of humanity entering this "second stage" of our collective "I" and the pain and disorder it has caused. And think about that diagnosis again: we are in this state *not able not to sin*.

After the fall of humanity, Gen 6:5 describes what God saw: "The Lord saw that the wickedness of man was great in the earth, and that every intention of the thoughts of his heart was only evil continually." How often do we hear about horrific news reports of what human beings can do to others human beings? Often when we all shake our heads, we might hear someone say, "How could someone do such a thing?" The answer? The second stage of humanity: we are not able not to sin. Thus, God proclaims our universal plight: "None is righteous, no, not one; no one understands; no one seeks for God" (Rom 3:10–11).

---

5. Elsewhere, I have expressed the considerable problem with the arbitrary idea that there are various "stages" that invite self-comparison to other believers (Espinosa, *Faith That Sees*, 113–15). Saint Augustine's distinctions are not this. Rather, Saint Augustine described a legitimate biblical anthropology: (1) man's state before the fall into sin, as both able to sin and able not to sin (*posse peccare, posse non peccare*); (2) after the fall into sin, as not able not to sin (*non posse non peccare*); (3) regenerated/converted man, as able not to sin (*posse non peccare*); (4) man in glory, as unable to sin (*non posse peccare*). Augustine, *Rebuke and Grace* 33 (*NPNF*[1] 5:485).

6. Augustine, *Enchiridion* 118 (*NPNF*[1] 3:275). The second stage describes sinful depravity and the significance of Eph 2:1–2a: "And you were dead in the trespasses and sins in which you once walked."

Contending for Identity: "I"

Now let's back up and think about this. Having entered this second "I" stage, *no matter what we do, we sin*. And here we should appreciate that the *condition of sin* (what we might call "core sin," or as the church calls it, "original sin") inevitably leads to the *thoughts, words, and actions of sin*. These are the behavioral results of core sin which the church calls "actual sins."

"No matter what we do, we sin," of course, can be highly offensive to some people, so what does Christian biblical theology mean by it? It does *not* mean that unbelievers or even Christians who act out in accord with their sinful nature (a very dangerous venture for the Christian, by the way) never do anything good and helpful in the civil realm. Of course they do, but the "good" that benefits the world is something God permits out of his mercy for all people. At the same time, if a person remains in this second stage "I," then all the "good" they do is never out of love for God, but for a "good" that is in some fashion ultimately "good" for the one doing it.

Christian ethics is entirely something else. Saint John put it simply, "We love because he first loved us" (1 John 4:19). The Christian does actual good not to be good but because God has been good to them. The Christian does good because they have been transformed by the love and mercy of God in Christ to reflect the goodness of Christ.

In the stage two "I," however, our preoccupation is self-service, even when we "serve" other people. Why? Because we are perpetually working out what is not right within us, and if we are doing this, then even while doing "good" to others, our "good" is self-aware and self-conscious about it. Even when what we do for others should be about others, it becomes about us.

And everyone in this real-life matrix just knows that something is wrong with that. We are consumed with ourselves because we know there is something wrong with us. No matter how hard people try, they keep doing things to alienate their relationship with God, hurt other people, and cause further damage to themselves. We know this happens. Often, we try to repress this awareness, sweep it under the rug, and pretend it isn't there, but we know it is there, and it won't go away.

Part I | First Article of the Creed

WHAT HAPPENS WHEN WE DON'T LIKE OUR "I"?

When we don't like ourselves and when we know that there is something wrong with ourselves, we do what comes naturally: we try to fix ourselves. And this is where life gets especially complicated.

One day when I was only a tween or so, my dear mother gave me a task, a job: "Alfonso, go out to the front yard with the clippers and trim that bush that is out of control." My assignment was clear. It was my mission, and I chose to accept it. Well, I had to since my mother told me to do it.

So, there I was: it was me and the bush, and before I knew it the whole affair became me *versus* the bush! I started to thoughtfully clip away. The funny thing about this project, however, was that my effort to sculpt a uniform shape just wasn't happening. Every time I thought I had one side just right, I realized the other side was still off. Before I knew it, I was going back and forth, never satisfied with my efforts for symmetry.

When my mother came out to check on my job, she was beside herself: "Alfonso, what have you done?!" The bush no longer even *looked* like a bush; it had become something else altogether. In fact, it was hardly recognizable.

I think you can see where this analogy is taking us. The reality is that we do this sort of thing all the time, not just on bushes but on *ourselves*. Because we sense something is wrong with us, we start clipping to find an identity that seems to correct that "wrong." As a result

- we might clip at our personalities,
- we might clip at our lifestyles,
- we might clip at our sexuality.

And just when we think the bush is starting to look right, we realize it isn't, so we clip some more. The vicious cycle leads many people to make drastic changes, believing that those changes will lead them to peace. After all, we all want to be "true" to ourselves, our instincts, and our consciences. But oftentimes after we have accomplished our major redoes, we don't find that peace we were striving for. The second stage "I" is still there, and our dissonance remains.

CONTENDING FOR IDENTITY: "I"

GOD'S PLAN FOR THIRD STAGE "I"

Nobody understands our predicament with second stage "I" better than God does. That shouldn't surprise us since he made us and fully sympathizes with our predicament. But let me back up a bit.

In going back to what happened during the first stage when our first parents had a choice, since they were "able to sin, able not to sin," was God just rolling the dice? We know that he wanted his people to genuinely love him as he genuinely loved them, but did he *know* what was going to happen?

Of course he did. He's God. There is this attribute of God called "omniscience" (all-knowingness) and that includes "foreknowledge." In other words, God knows exactly what is going to happen before it happens.[7] The fact that God *knew* what was going to happen, however, doesn't mean that God *caused* it to happen. No, that was *our* doing, not God's. But still, if God knew, why didn't he do something about it? And here when this question is asked, it betrays a humongous cultural assumption that God didn't. *But he did*. His word teaches,

> In love he predestined us for adoption to himself as sons through Jesus Christ, according to the purpose of his will, to the praise of his glorious grace, with which he has blessed us in the Beloved. In him we have redemption through his blood, the forgiveness of our trespasses, according to the riches of his grace, which he lavished upon us, in all wisdom and insight making known to us the mystery of his will, according to his purpose, which he set forth in Christ as a plan for the fullness of time, to unite all things in heaven and things on earth. (Eph 1:4b–10)

God had very much done something about our rebellion and our fall from stage one "I" to stage two "I." What he did about it was promise the redeeming and healing ministry of his Son, Jesus Christ, so that we would not remain stuck with our messed-up "I," nor would we be stuck in the endless cycle of never getting our clipping right.

---

7. It is important, however, that we do not confuse foreknowledge with determinism. The fact that God *knows* something will happen before it happens *does not mean that God causes that thing to happen*. What is closer to the truth is not hard determinism, but compatibilism, which is a real-life combination of nothing happening that God does not permit to happen, while we are responsible for our second stage "I" rebellion against God. God doesn't make anyone sin, but rather we choose to sin.

Part I | First Article of the Creed

THIRD STAGE "I": A GREAT "I" TO BE

Don't look now, but we have arrived at the "I" of the Apostles' Creed! Among the four stages we have been tracking, stage three describes a human being who through conversion to Christ is now "able not to sin."

Unlike the stage one condition, the person in stage three *has sinned and possesses a core sin nature / sinful nature* that is always inclined towards sin. In fact, this core sin nature causes the converted Christian to constantly sin in weakness.[8] In this respect, anyone in stage three is constantly sinning and not simply in possession of core sin. However, the person in stage three is no longer captive to sin, as is the case in stage two.

It becomes especially significant, therefore, that a person at stage two (not able not to sin) transitions to stage three (able not to sin). The difference in fact is earthshaking and indicative that Christ has entered someone's life. Jesus described stage three this way: "Truly, truly, I say to you, whoever hears my word and believes him who sent me has eternal life. He does not come into judgment but has passed from death to life" (John 5:24).

Stage three, however, is not a walk in the park. It is rather a constant battle between the sinful nature and the born-again spirit.[9] Yes, a kind of internal "off-ness"—in respect to the inner battle or conflict (Rom 7, Gal 5)—is the normal Christian experience.

The inner conflict at stage three, however, is completely recognizable and understood, unlike the stage two condition which is primed to lead a person to self-destruction. And while no one can fathom the dark depths of the sinful nature, at least the Christian knows *why* they struggle as they do, they know *how* that struggle often manifests, and most importantly, they know—finally!—*what* has been done and continues to be done about it by God.

These insights bring about a new spirit, liberation for the soul, and freedom from bondage to sin. The stage three "I" is a new "I" that knows that God's word is not only the foundation for truth in life but also that

---

8. Thus, the Christian church practices constant confession and absolution in both corporate and individual settings. This is consistent with the teaching in God's word recorded at 1 John 1:8–9: "If we say we have no sin, we deceive ourselves, and the truth is not in us. If we confess our sins, he is faithful and just to forgive us our sins and to cleanse us from all unrighteousness."

9. See my first book (Espinosa, *Faith That Sees*, ch. 7, ["The Lutheran Lens—What Am I?"]) which elaborates upon the inner conflict of the Christian, which God uses for the good of the Christian.

which acts as a guide for life to help us see what we would never see on our own (Ps 119:105). And even when we think we see (John 9:41), the word of God corrects us, keeping us humble to walk by faith and not by sight (2 Cor 5:7).

THIRD STAGE "I" KNOWS TWO "I'S" IN ONE PERSON

Through his servant and apostle Saint Paul, the Lord granted even deeper insight into the complexity of stage three. God provides keen insight into the experiential dynamics of the "I" (or rather the "I's") at stage three. Saint Paul wrote, "I have been crucified with Christ. It is no longer I who live, but Christ lives in me. And the life I now live in the flesh I live by faith in the Son of God, who loved me and gave himself for me" (Gal 2:20).

A straightforward and yet profound teaching is presented here. The apostle is describing that his person consists of two "I's." He referred to the first "I" by writing,

"*I* have been crucified with Christ. It is no longer *I* who live."

And then he continued by writing about the second "I,"

"And the life *I* now live in the flesh *I live* by faith in the Son of God."

Stage three represents the person who is a Christian, born from above through Holy Baptism and faith in Jesus Christ. This Christian in stage three has two "I's": the "I" that came into stage three from stage two; and the new "I," introduced through spiritual rebirth. This stage three "I," comprised of the two "I's," is the first word of the Apostles' Creed.

Luther wrote, "Christ . . . is fixed and cemented to me and abides in Me. The life that I now live, He lives in me. Indeed, Christ Himself is the life that I now live. In this way, therefore, Christ and I are one."[10]

This new "I," therefore, represents a new life in Christ. While the old "I" still hangs around in the sinful nature, it no longer defines the Christian. In stage three, sin is no longer the master of the person. Saint Paul writes elsewhere, "For sin will have no dominion over you, since you are not under law but under grace" (Rom 6:14).

And most importantly, when God looks upon the Christian, he does not see the old "I" but the new, essential "I," the lasting "I," the "I" in Christ, the "I" that determines the lasting identity of the man or woman in Christ.

---

10. Luther, *Galatians*, 167.

Saint Augustine understood how to keep the two "I's" at stage three in proper relationship: "For where I am not I, I am more happily I."[11]

CHAPTER 1 DISCUSSION GUIDE: CONTENDING FOR IDENTITY: "I"

UNCOVER INFORMATION

1. What is the first stage "I"?
2. What is the second stage "I"?
3. What is the third stage "I"?
4. What are the two "I's" within third stage "I"?
5. Which of the two "I's" within third stage "I" is predominant in the baptized Christian?

DISCOVER MEANING

1. Why did humanity transition from first stage "I" to second stage "I"?
2. In second stage "I," what do we mean by people knowing that something is off?
3. On our own, apart from Christ, what do we do with the sense of "off-ness"?
4. If someone says that God is to blame for second stage "I," how might we give an answer?
5. What did Luther and Augustine mean by their respective quotations in this chapter?

EXPLORE IMPLICATIONS

1. What kind of "good works" do people in second stage "I" perform, if they do perform them?
2. Why do people "start clipping" within second stage "I"? How might the Christian respond?

---

11. Edwards, *Galatians, Ephesians, Philippians*, 32.

3. Since God sent his Son to rescue us from second stage "I," how ought we respond in third stage "I"?

4. Since the Christian is "able not to sin," in third stage "I," how should the Christian view this state?

5. Considering Gal 2:20, how might the Christian view the daily battle/conflict between the two "I's" in a positive way?

2

Culture and the Old "I"

"*I believe* . . . " but the world doesn't.

ENTER THE CULTURE

Having laid the foundation regarding the four stages of "I," the Christian church must contend for the faith considering how the culture appeals to the old "I" in all people whether they find themselves at stage two or three. But if we have identified this problem as an internal one, then why concern ourselves with considerations about the external culture?

When confessing the articles of faith about the causation of sin, the Christian church is thorough. Sin (the condition of being turned in on oneself and living in hostility towards God) comes from three causes:

1. Human nature
2. The world
3. Satan

Suffice it to say that the three causes of sin work together. To demonstrate the interrelationship between internal and external aspects, consider the famous psychological experiment: Pavlov's dogs and the Pavlovian conditioning response. The psychological experiment demonstrated that dogs could be conditioned to salivate at the sound of a bell indicating food was coming. In this analogy we are the salivating canines. The "bell" is the

Culture and the Old "I"

world and the devil pulling us towards reaction and interaction, the carrying out of what is already in the heart of people (i.e., sin).

Part and parcel of contending for the faith is to understand how the world and the devil are active in the culture (not at all to say that everything in the culture is bad, most certainly not). And these enemies of God are dedicated to deception.

It is hard to think of a made-for-television franchise that has had so many versions of it produced like that of *Star Trek*. A long time ago, I lost track of the order of its various versions, but this much I know: the second *Star Trek* series was *The Next Generation* with Captain Picard, his first officer, "Number One," and of course his second officer, "Data."

I was personally underwhelmed by the series, but there was a subset of episodes I found fascinating. It was when the Starship *Enterprise* was flung far into the deepest quadrants of the galaxy to encounter none other than the almost invincible aliens called the "Borg," an intimidating and frightful bunch to say the least.

They were cyborgs and were fond of asserting to everyone they set out to "assimilate," "Resistance is futile."[1] They even managed to kidnap Captain Picard and turn him into one of their own. Of course, he was rescued and through *Star Trek* biotechnology was restored to the Captain Picard of old.

But I digress. There was just one point of illustration here pertinent to our current consideration of the world and the devil interacting with human core sin: what was so fascinating about the Borg is that they were programmed and able to adapt to enemy attack (such as *Star Trek* energy weapons) and furthermore, were experts at regeneration while adapting new tactics.

I find these Borg-like qualities a fictional analogy of what the world and Satan do with the sin in the hearts and minds of people. It is assuredly true that "there is nothing new" (the same key players which instigate sin are always there), but at the same time, they dress up in the latest fashion.

THE DEVIL AND THE WORLD SHAPE-SHIFT

The world and the devil are always shape-shifting to catch people off guard so that they might suppress their concern about what is missing and what is wrong. In this way, people might become consumed with the latest versions of false promises leading to destruction.

---

1. Bole, "Best of Both Worlds."

We see a microcosm of this multifaceted, shape-shifting worldly and satanic strategy in our Lord's wilderness temptation by the devil. Luke records the steps the devil took to try to tempt Jesus:

- First, he went after Jesus' identity—"If you are the Son of God, command this stone to become bread" (Luke 4:3). This was a psychological temptation.
- Then the devil tried to elicit the desire for power and possession—"To you I will give all this authority and their glory" (Luke 4:6). This was a sociological or status temptation.
- And finally, the devil used the word of God itself to lure Jesus to test the word instead of trusting in it(Luke 4:9–11). This was a religious or spiritual temptation.

The world and the devil use the same core temptations for pride, money, sex, power, etc. so that the sin in the human heart might be unleashed. (Although it will find a way to get out all by itself, the world and the devil are happy to make it worse.) What is the goal of human core sin + worldly influence in the culture + demonic influence?

1. That people will spend much less time realizing that there is something wrong within themselves as they become immersed (and sometimes obsessed) with worldly pursuits.
2. That people would give free reign to their sin already within their hearts. In this case, sin would become totally consuming while the world and Satan treat that sin as perfectly normal.
3. That people would be cut off from the saving gospel of the Lord Jesus Christ. (This, of course, is the most serious threat from the enemies against humanity.) The devil wants to destroy, and the best way to do this is to take away the hope of the gospel of Jesus Christ from a person's soul.

THE CONTENDING CHRISTIAN MUST READ THE CURRENT CULTURE

Negative threats in the culture are seen through the lens of the word of God. Whatever the culture denies, contradicts, rejects, and/or tries to substitute for God's word must be confronted by the Christian who will "contend for the faith that was once for all delivered to the saints" (Jude 3). The Christian cannot permit the faith that is founded upon the word of Christ to be compromised.

Again, this does not mean the Christian is to be contentious, argumentative, defensive, rude, and certainly not obnoxious towards those who hold a different worldview or faith. In fact, as I have also said above, the Christian is a light for Christ and his love, even (and especially) in the face of enemies.[2]

This contending Christian must furthermore discern the negative threats in the culture which seek to accommodate, facilitate, and perpetuate the sin in the heart, the evil in the world, and the attacks of the devil. In doing so, the Christian is in a better position to contend intelligently while loving their neighbor who holds worldviews contrary to eternal life in Christ.

The twentieth century in America saw unique cultural circumstances that easily brought out the worst of humanity and the world. Satan had plenty of opportunity to add to the chaos through world wars, extreme poverty, racism with civil unrest, the removal of prayer from public schools, the sexual revolution, the 1973 invention of the cell phone, the 1983 invention of the internet, and the 1992 invention of the smartphone.

Take the whole list and mix it with the spiritual influences of the world and the demonic and watch out. Even something like the smartphone, designed to help people, can morph into another addiction or portal through which a person's identity enters a chaotic state. With every new thing, the potential for a new spiritual prison comes with it.

Can any of these things be used for good? Of course they can and, by God's mercy, are. However, the point here is that the Christian who would contend for the faith must know what's going on in the culture and then consider its interaction with principalities and powers (Eph 6:12). And this battle is not about Christians fighting those who believe differently but is rather the *spiritual* battle behind the scenes against sin itself: in the human heart, the world, and the devil.

CULTURE AND GOD'S GOOD SEXUALITY

One of the easiest ways to try to cover up our inner sense that something is off and wrong is to rush headlong into preoccupation or even obsession

---

2. Espinosa, *Faith That Shines*.

with our sexuality. And like my tween face-off with the bush, we get out our clippers, and with that one stroke of presumption, we assume it is okay to start clipping. Before we know it, we can enter an endless cycle of recalibrations and fateful explorations.

It should be said at the forefront that all people do this in some way, degree, or fashion. No one is innocent of our insistence to treat our bodies as canvasses to be painted upon or objects for increasing sexual stimulation. We do it in varying degrees through

- exercise programs and regiments to sculpt our bodies;
- plastic surgery;
- cosmetics, especially when combined with long swaths of time in front of mirrors;
- implants;
- tattoos;
- eating too little or eating too much;
- various examples of violating the sixth commandment;
- transsexuality.

And as we await the second coming of our Lord, the list will only get longer. With the coming surge of AI and biotechnology, we will also have to increasingly contend with

- sexual activity in tandem with AI life-like human facsimiles;
- the incorporation of technology upon, within, and extending from the human body.

In all these things there is one grand assumption in the culture: the person's body is *their* body in a cultural milieu breeding hyper-individualism, relativism, and skepticism towards any truth-claim that is not one's own.[3] That is, our bodies and sexuality are whatever we say they are. This streams from the nonsensical and illogical belief that "there are no moral absolutes," as this is absolutely applied to morality.

But such a self-aggrandizing idea about our identities, bodies, and sexuality is hatched from the off-ness known within our souls. This

---

3. Espinosa, *Faith That Engages*, 48–50, 183–84.

presumption that our bodies belong exclusively to us is the first step towards destroying or at least significantly causing damage to the bush.

While speaking to his stage three people, God says, "Or do you not know that your body is a temple of the Holy Spirit within you, whom you have from God? You are not your own, for you were bought with a price. So glorify God in your body" (1 Cor 6:19–20).

My body is not my own. As a baptized Christian man, my body is God's body. Even the house I live in, whose mortgage I'm making good progress toward paying off, is not my house, and it won't even be when (God permitting) it is all paid for. It is from God, and God desires I manage it to glorify him and serve others. The same is true of my bodily house.

In fact, there is even another owner of my body—namely, my wife, Traci. God says, "For the wife does not have authority over her own body, but the husband does. Likewise, the husband does not have authority over his own body, but the wife does" (1 Cor 7:4).

But the sinful forces in the world and the devil act upon the culture, and presumptions about our identities, bodies, and sexualities come cascading down upon us. What the temptations, delusions, and lies have in common, however, is the claim again that our bodies are *not* from God.

So, if our bodies do not belong to God (nor anyone else), then it must be all about me and, of course, what "I" want (the problem with stage two "I"). Sin wants to convince us, "Do what you please with your body. Mold it, tailor it, paint it, change it, do what you will. It is all yours." This pattern in the world is the same for the formation of identity. The questions "Who am I?" and "What am I?" are crucial questions to properly answer. However, the answer in the culture today is utterly self-serving and relativistic: "Whatever you say!" or, perhaps for those whose confidence is waning, "Whatever the culture says!" Indeed, the world and the devil have no trouble offering their views about who and what we are. In every case those answers are destructive, driving us further from God who created us, the Savior who redeemed us, and the Holy Spirit who desires to guide and comfort us.

CONTENDING WITH WISDOM

The *New York Times* journalist Pamela Paul wrote an eye-opening opinion piece entitled, "As Kids, They Thought They Were Trans. They No Longer Do."[4] I was struck how something written in 2024 from a popular secular

---

4. Paul, "As Kids."

source could so powerfully present the incredible crisis that is transitioning and the frequent attempts to detransition. The personal and real-life testimonies in the opinion piece are heart-wrenching. I was not, however, given permission to include these in this volume, so I had to look elsewhere for real people sharing the horrendous experiences they've had.

Dr. Ryan T. Anderson's book, *When Harry Became Sally: Responding to the Transgender Moment* is effective in exposing and refuting the fallacies of the idea in our culture today that it is possible to "transition" from one gender to another.

Transgenderism finds its underpinnings in gender dysphoria when a person feels a tremendous mismatch between their biological sex—male and female—and how they perceive or identify themselves other than their biological selves. Dr. Anderson alerts us to the tremendous need to treat the identity crisis with compassion and understanding: "People with gender dysphoria don't choose it and aren't faking it. They really are suffering. And we should take their testimony seriously."[5]

At the same time, we must also take seriously the mistaken solution of transitioning, which Anderson further describes:

> In 2007, Boston Children's Hospital "became the first major program in the United States to focus on transgender children and adolescents," as its website brags. A decade later, more than forty-five pediatric gender clinics had opened their doors to our nation's children. Parents are told that puberty blockers and cross-sex hormones may be the only way to prevent their children from committing suicide.[6]

The popular and errant presumption is that suicidal ideation can be countered by gender transitioning. After hormonal therapy comes "surgery to alter primary and secondary sex characteristics."[7] The damage done is now well known.

> For many people, surgery does well as a cosmetic matter, but a botched surgery led this anonymous author to question what she was doing in the first place. And as she notes in her narrative, the medical professionals never provided any counseling to help her understand why she felt so strongly that she wanted to be a man. "I

---

5. Anderson, *When Harry Became Sally*, xii.
6. Anderson, *When Harry Became Sally*, 2.
7. Anderson, *When Harry Became Sally*, 34.

had assumed the problem was in my body. Now I saw that it wasn't being female that was stopping me from being myself."[8]

And yet another testifier stated, "I detransitioned because I knew I could not continue running from myself, dissociating myself, because acknowledging my reality as a woman is vital to my mental health."[9] This same person could look back on her gender dysphoria and say, "It wasn't just you know, some innate identity [but] . . . it was a maladaptive coping mechanism for me."[10]

As opposed to what is maladaptive and misleading, the word of God offers clarity as opposed to the deceptions of our core sin, the world, and the devil. What is a man and what is male, and what is a woman and what is female, has been given to us from above.

The problem within the culture, however, is that it has strayed from biblical estates and vocations which help us to recognize men as men and women as women. For example, what happens today if the standard for femininity for a young lady is a Victoria's Secret model?[11] The challenge for achieving a healthy self-identity includes considering what our culture is doing to compound the off-ness that is already present within the soul. A young woman may struggle with her identity as a woman, believing she must fit into the cultural expectation of an ideal woman. If she is detached from the word of God, we should not be surprised that her identity struggles will be exacerbated by potentially misleading or even dangerous cultural versions of gender.

CHRISTIANS WHO CONTEND AND WHO CARE

For any young person going through gender dysphoria, the church needs to practice the way of Christ towards that person. And what is that, in this instance? It is always these things:

---

8. Anderson, *When Harry Became Sally*, 50.
9. Anderson, *When Harry Became Sally*, 53.
10. Anderson, *When Harry Became Sally*, 54.
11. We do not cast blame on professional models but rather on the potential images of womanhood or manhood which become predominant—promulgated by the culture—upon young psyches.

1. Compassion—Christians extend their hearts to care about anyone struggling with the various manifestations of what is wrong within themselves and the world.

2. Empathy—Christians are called to "Rejoice with those who rejoice, weep with those who weep" (Rom 12:15).

3. Sympathy—Christians come alongside anyone struggling with their off-ness by helping to bear the load of whatever is causing the suffering. Christians suffer with those who suffer, in love.

The church must also be cognizant that when a person is this brittle, ransacked by their own shame and confusion, and bombarded by a culture making it worse, the last thing this person needs is the church resorting to legalism and moralism. What is needed first are Christians who will simply love the person who is suffering, listen to them, and invest in that relationship that they might be as Christ to them, as well as see the amazing grace of God which permits the person being served to be as Christ back to the Christian (Matt 25:40). But what does the gospel really offer this person already heavy-laden by the accusations of the law? It offers how the Lord sees them right through the eyes of Jesus.

In 1966 Patricia McGerr published a short story in an issue of the *Australian Women's Weekly*.[12] She told the story of Johnny Lingo who voyaged from his Pacific Island of Narabundi to the island of Kiniwata to find his future wife. In Kiniwata, suitors bartered and offered cows to the father's daughters on the island. Two or three cows were offered for an average wife, but four or five for an exceptional one. But Johnny offered the father of his beloved Sarita eight cows, a number that no one on the island could fathom.

Johnny Lingo saw something no one else could see. He saw what Sarita could be. He poured out grace upon her. The story, of course, falls short of reality, as most illustrations and analogies do. If we sinners are Sarita, we can claim no hidden potential or concealed beauty. Sin leads to death. However, as sin is more severe than hidden beauty, Christ's saving work is infinitely greater than betting on hidden potential. Christ dawns upon those in a darkness they could not otherwise ever escape.

Christ is the husband of the holy church, and he creates in all her members a new, essential "I." It is his gift to his bride. *His* light upon us

---

12. McGerr, "Johnny Lingo."

makes us shine with a radiance both brilliant and beautiful beyond words. Jesus—by grace—makes us beautiful through faith in him.

CONTENDING FOR THE BRIDEGROOM, HUSBAND, AND FATHER

Christians can contend for the faith once delivered by not only rejecting the lies that seek to destroy lives, but through engaging people so that they might know *the* bridegroom, the most excellent *Husband* who paid the price no one else could pay.

This reality, however, cannot be only a religious meditation; it needs to come to the fore in real life. Christians are called to live this truth out, especially in the family, and especially through the spiritual leadership of men who would be faithful husbands and faithful fathers.

After all, when dads train up their little girls to know they are beautiful, gifted, and intelligent, and that their sons are strong young men who can do and will do great things, then the children not only take on a confidence about what they might accomplish, but about who they already are: beloved children.

The Israelites' approach to medicine and healthcare emphasized *prevention*. You might know the old saying, "An ounce of prevention is worth a pound of cure." The church does not have to wait for crises, they may instead focus on serving families to walk together, pray together, worship together, and affirm together. In this way, body, gender, and all other dysphorias might be covered by love.

This love is not hidden away. It is rather revealed. We have a heavenly Father who loves all of us this way. And so the creed continues, "I . . . believe in God, the Father almighty."

That is, the creed contends with the culture for the faith once delivered so that the culture's insistence upon false gods might give way to the God who can be known, the heavenly Father. There are reasons that may be demonstrated in loving contention that if God is knowable and makes it clear that he desires to be known, then when we know him, we might finally know ourselves and find the peace and joy we have been looking for. To the next part of the creed we now turn.

CHAPTER 2 DISCUSSION GUIDE: CULTURE AND THE OLD "I"

UNCOVER INFORMATION

1. Being turned in on oneself and living in hostility toward God comes from what three things?
2. How are the world and the devil illustrated by the Borg?
3. What is meant by "shape-shifting" in this chapter?
4. What is meant by the Christian "reading" the culture?
5. What does the culture say about sexuality?

DISCOVER MEANING

1. How does the analogy of Pavlov's dogs help explain the interaction between sin, on the one hand, and the world and the devil, on the other?
2. The fact that Satan tempted Jesus in three very different ways teaches us what about the ways of the devil?
3. Describe the world's and Satan's goals against people through worldly and Satanic influence.
4. What is so dangerous about the idea that our bodies belong to us alone?
5. What is the point of contending for the faith with wisdom?

EXPLORE IMPLICATIONS

1. Read 1 John 2:15–16. How should Christians abide in this instruction while living in the world?
2. In the face of the world's and Satan's strategies against us, what ought the Christian do, especially regarding these specific attacks?
3. New inventions are exciting, but how might they threaten people in the face of the spiritual battle?
4. Since our bodies ultimately belong to God, how should we treat them?
5. What are the implications for the church in respect to the story of Johnny Lingo and Sarita?

3

Contending for the Father

"I believe in God, **the Father** Almighty."

WHERE IS GOD?

When one considers the expanse of the universe, it is overwhelmingly humbling. Our planet compared to the universe is smaller than the period at the end of this sentence when compared to the length of this book. How much less may a person's existence seem in the broad expanse of the universe? We are smaller than a speck of dust in the wind or a granule of sand on the seashore compared to the size of the universe. And when someone is this inordinately small, it is easy to be skeptical about a God who cares about us, if indeed he exists at all. Why would he care for someone so small, and why presume he exists?

Taking this into consideration, it seems like a stretch that he would care about us. It might make more sense to call it for what it might seem to be: "God" is a figment of our imagination. Maybe the famous atheist Richard Dawkins is right to say that believing in God qualifies as a delusion.[1]

What might be surprising to some, however, is that God himself is completely aware of how people react to the appearance of our universe:

> When I look at your heavens, the work of your fingers, the moon and the stars, which you have set in place, what is man that you

---

1. Dawkins, *God Delusion*.

are mindful of him, and the son of man that you care for him? (Ps 8:3–4)

As for the more extreme position that God does not even exist, that too is covered in God's word. He teaches us that Satan's activity comes

> with all wicked deception for those who are perishing, because they refused to love the truth and so be saved. Therefore God sends them a strong delusion, so that they may be condemned who did not believe the truth but had pleasure in unrighteousness. (2 Thess 2:10–12)

This "strong delusion" may very well include the exasperated inability to see the God who is there. But why would God ever send a strong delusion?

In addition to his love and mercy, God is also just, and he uses his justice to extend his mercy. If anyone hardens their heart (Prov 28:14) and suppresses the truth (Rom 1:18), then God obliges their rebellion against him. God is *just* in the face of their rebellion. But when he is, his mercy also remains fully intact because he *always* "desires all people to be saved and to come to the knowledge of the truth" (1 Tim 2:4).

Why then does he permit some to continue to reject him? So that, perhaps, they might be able to give similar testimony later in their lives, as Saint Paul did:

> I thank him who has given me strength, Christ Jesus our Lord, because he judged me faithful, appointing me to his service, though formerly I was a blasphemer, persecutor, and insolent opponent. But I received mercy because I had acted ignorantly in unbelief, and the grace of our Lord overflowed for me with the faith and love that are in Christ Jesus. The saying is trustworthy and deserving of full acceptance, that Christ Jesus came into the world to save sinners, of whom I am the foremost. But I received mercy for this reason, that in me, as the foremost, Jesus Christ might display his perfect patience as an example to those who were to believe in him for eternal life. To the King of the ages, immortal, invisible, the only God, be honor and glory forever and ever. Amen. (1 Tim 1:12–17)

Still, it is so hard to see God in our lives. Any skepticism about the God question is not helped by conditions here on planet earth. Jesus predicted what would occur (and is occurring) in this world: "And you will hear of wars and rumors of wars.... Nation will rise against nation, and there will be famines and earthquakes in various places. . . . Lawlessness will be increased, the love of many will grow cold" (Matt 24:6, 7, 12).

Saint Paul, likewise, depressingly elaborated on the last days in which we are currently living:[2]

> People will be lovers of self, lovers of money, proud, arrogant, abusive, disobedient to their parents, ungrateful, unholy, heartless, unappeasable, slanderous, without self-control, brutal, not loving good, treacherous, reckless, swollen with conceit, lovers of pleasure rather than lovers of God, having the appearance of godliness, but denying its power. (2 Tim 3:2–5)

And we have not even touched the surface of disease and all that attacks our bodies, nor have we yet mentioned the incredible heartbreak that occurs when we lose loved ones who die too soon. Who can account for this pain, which has driven one of the most devastating arguments against God in the history of the world? David Hume elucidated upon his understanding of the argument—the so-called "problem of evil"—as originally put forth by Epicurus:

> *Epicurus's* old questions are yet unanswered. Is [God] willing to prevent evil, but not able? then he is impotent. Is he able, but not willing? then he is malevolent. Is he both able and willing? whence then is evil?[3]

This question has driven people to push back against God as their souls scream, "Where are you?!" While I was still a very young seminarian serving in my field work placement, I was assigned to the cancer ward at a local hospital. No amount of classroom training could have prepared me for what awaited me there.

On one occasion I walked into a man's room whose body was wrecked by and filled with cancer. He was writhing in pain as if on fire. It was a horrific real-life scene. As I opened my mouth to tell him why I was there—in some vain attempt to make a difference—he shouted at me, "Get out!" I was introduced to the feeling of total ineptitude.

At the same hospital, I went to visit a woman dying of cancer. She was fully cognizant and able to converse. I tried to bring some comfort, but

---

2. The Christian church has been living in the last days for two millennia, not just because a thousand years are as a day to God (2 Pet 3:8) but also so that every person might repent and come to the knowledge of the truth (2 Tim 2:25).

3. Hume, *Dialogues*, 108–9. We must rely upon secondary witnesses of the words of Epicurus as no primary sources of this quote by him exist.

there it was on her nightstand in the hospital room: the picture of her very young daughter she was preparing to leave behind. As bad as her cancer was, it could not match the pain in her heart for what was about to happen, not so much to her but to her daughter, soon to lose her loving mother. The short exchange we had didn't go very well.

Even for people who fully acknowledge and follow God, life can *still* be full of excruciating pain. But it is perhaps through these painful experiences we learn the most. This was true for one of my elders in my first congregational assignment as a young pastor.

The elder was a seasoned leader in the congregation and one of her most dedicated servants. He was elderly when we met and had been giving glory to God through a dedication rarely seen in the world. But why was he so remarkable to me?

Many years before we ever met, he was enjoying a pleasant outing with the love of his life. He and his wife had gone out to a local grocery store. What happened that day was a nightmare come to life. An armed robber entered the grocery store. He fired off a round. The stray bullet found his wife, and she died in her husband's arms.

When my elder told me about what he had experienced, a recounting that still brought tears to his eyes many years after he lost his wife to this insane injustice, he did it in such a way that demonstrated he was filled with the wisdom of God. He spoke as Job once did: "Shall we receive good from God, and shall we not receive evil?" (Job 2:10). Although God is not the author of evil, he permits the suffering from evil even upon his very own, which my elder well knew. It is for this reason alone that many people have either left the Christian faith or have never come to it.

But there was One who knew this better than anyone ever did, and this, too, my elder knew. This One was perfectly united to the Father, completely One with him, and forged with the Father and the Holy Spirit in perfect love. Yet this One who knew perfect oneness with the Father also knew the most terrible suffering the world had ever known, crucified on a Roman cross.[4] While he was dying, he could no longer see God. Where had his Father gone?

---

4. Not only was Roman execution among the most meticulously planned ways in the history of the world to kill a man torturously, maximizing the most suffering over many hours, but while Christ was dying on the cross, he permitted himself to know the sins of the world upon himself.

Better than anyone before or after him, he knew what it was like not to see God. He cried out from the cross, *"Eli, Eli, lema sabachthani?"*—that is, "My God, my God, why have you forsaken me?" (Matt 27:46).

Epicurus was essentially asserting through his argument against God, "He has not done anything about the evil in the world." But *nothing* could be further from the truth. The Father saw to it that it was exactly to the contrary: he sent the world his one and only Son, the Lord Jesus Christ (John 3:16). This is something that he had prepared to do from the very foundations of the world (Eph 1:4).

OUR FATHER HAS NEVER LEFT AND WILL NEVER LEAVE

Sin, the world, and the devil try hard to attack the Father's reputation, especially while attacking earthly fathers and the family. I have argued that among the three major estates—family, congregation, and state—(not counting the estate of love which flows through these three) that the most important one is the family estate.[5] And within this indispensable estate is the vocation/call for men to be fathers, faithful fathers.

But how often is this not the case? Whether fathers forsake their home altogether or stay and abuse their family, they leave.[6] And when fathers abandon what it means to be faithful fathers, everyone in the family suffers from it. Wives and mothers are betrayed and children grow up with the word "father" not conjuring what is good but what is exceedingly negative.

Families are under attack, and the best way to begin to hurt a family is through a father who himself does not know the heavenly Father. For myself, I was blessed to have a dad who was always there for me. Even to this day, his example emblazoned upon my memory—long after his death—continues to bless me, and I give thanks to my heavenly Father for him.

But despite the many shortcomings of our earthly fathers, there is a Father who doesn't have any. He is the Father who never leaves. He is there and available twenty-four seven, supplying all our needs for our body and life. By "life," we mean for *all* aspects of life and for *every* need.

It is easy to miss the significance of John 3:16 when it comes to our Father in heaven. When it begins with the words, "For God so loved the

---

5. Espinosa, *Faith That Shines*.
6. Both physical abandonment and emotional abandonment can be equally devastating to families. Both forms constitute the forsaking of spiritual leadership which the Lord desires for families to know stability, healing, and love.

world that he gave his only Son," "God," in this glorious gospel, or good news, refers to God the Father. The word for "love" is sacrificial love that gave what was most precious to himself, his only begotten Son to save us from sin and death.

"Only begotten" might sound strange to some, but it is a descriptor of just how close the Father was and is to the Son. Jesus is the Son of God, which is another way of saying that Jesus *is* God, because "Son of God" in this instance is a title of divinity. He is very God of very God.[7]

These words in the creed, "only begotten," teach about the relationship between the Father who is God and the Son who is God and how they are perfectly One.[8] "Only begotten" means Jesus is the unique and one-of-a-kind Son of the Father. He is an eternal extension of the Father, and they are never separate but always One. While the Father always loves his Son, the Son always gives glory to his Father, faithful to him also in perfect love.

When we understand the significance of "only begotten," we start to realize the enormity of what the Father did for *us*. In the most wondrous love the world has ever known, the Father loved *us* so much that he gave us what was most dear and important to himself. And a Father who loves *this much* has never and will never abandon us.

Moses spoke these words to Israel: "Be strong and courageous. Do not fear or be in dread of [your enemies], for it is the Lord your God who goes with you. He will not leave you or forsake you" (Deut 31:6). Much later in time, King David said to Solomon his son, "Be strong and courageous and [build the temple of God]. Do not be afraid and do not be dismayed, for the Lord God, even my God, is with you. He will not leave you or forsake you, until all the work for the service of the house of the Lord is finished" (1 Chr 28:20). The author of the book of Hebrews applies these promises to all who follow Christ: "For [God] has said, 'I will never leave you nor forsake you.'" And then he says in the very next verse, "So we can confidently say, 'The Lord is my helper; I will not fear; what can man do to me?'" (Heb 13:5–6).

To put it simply, if the Father loved us so much that he gave the greatest love in his life—his only Son—for us, he is not about to leave or abandon us.

---

7. As the holy church confesses in the Nicene Creed.

8. Christianity is falsely accused of not teaching monotheism (that God is One), but Father, Son, and Holy Spirit should never be thought of in terms of $1 + 1 + 1 = 3$, but rather $1 \times 1 \times 1 = 1$. Christians confess that the "who" of God is Father, Son, and Holy Spirit, and that the "what" of God is that he is One essence or substance.

So, where do we find God? We find him in his Son, Jesus Christ. And when we find Jesus, what does he teach us? That God, our Father, will never leave us nor will he ever forsake us. Jesus teaches us that in truth the Father loves us more than we can possibly imagine. Then why doesn't the Father make his love for us plainer to see?

THE FATHER KNOWS HOW HE SHOULD BE SEEN

It should be stated up front that many people only think they know how God ought to make himself better known, and overestimate their potential change of heart if God would cater to their expectations.

Jesus once addressed people's misplaced optimism about themselves when he told the parable about the rich man and Lazarus. The rich man who was in hell and who had lived only for himself while on earth was in a dialogue with Abraham in heaven. The rich man begged Abraham to send Lazarus, also in heaven, back to earth to warn the rich man's brothers about the terrible fate that awaited them if they did not repent of their sins. The rich man in hell asserted his overestimation of human capacity:

> But Abraham said, "They [the rich man's brothers on earth] have Moses and the Prophets; let them hear them." And [the rich man in hell] said, "No, father Abraham, but if someone goes to them from the dead, they will repent." [Abraham replied], "If they do not hear Moses and the Prophets, neither will they be convinced if someone should rise from the dead." (Luke 16:29–31)

The rich man had fully convinced himself that he knew exactly what God should permit to be better known. He was wrong. The core sin problem in man is so devastating that God could drop a sign down from heaven, and people would explain why the sign was not from God.

Nobody knows the situation better than the heavenly Father, so he proceeds in such a way for us to arrive at the point of learning that the child of God must live by their faith and not by their sight (2 Cor 5:7). This must be true because what we see with our physical eyes is easily misconstrued.

Peter Kreeft provides an analogy that begins to explain how our perception of God and knowledge of his ways fall short. Despite our dullness, however, what God demonstrates is always for our good even when we are convinced that it couldn't possibly be:

Imagine a bear in a trap and a hunter who, out of sympathy, wants to liberate him. He tries to win the bears confidence but he can't do it, so he has to shoot the bear full of drugs. The bear, however, thinks this is an attack and that the hunter is trying to kill him. He doesn't realize that this is being done out of compassion. Then in order to get the bear out of the trap, the hunter has to push him further into the trap to release the tension on the spring. If the bear were semiconscious at that point, he would be even more convinced that the hunter was his enemy who was out to cause him suffering and pain. But the bear would be wrong. He reaches this incorrect conclusion because he's not a human being.[9]

It is easy to see God as the hunter who only causes pain, but our eyes deceive us, and our reason falls short of grasping how God accomplishes good even through the evil and suffering that is in the world. We only think we know the best way for God the Father to show himself to us, but this is not so.

John Bloom, one of my most gifted professors, once explained the "sheriff's in town" effect related to our current consideration.[10] What if it was painfully clear beyond a shadow of a doubt that God was in our midst, obvious to everyone on earth? Then yes, many, if not most, people would change their ways, but would those behavioral adjustments mean that these same people would love God and trust in him? Or would their conceding to his presence only cloak anything but true faith, truly holding to him and trusting in him more than anything else in the universe?

Sometimes people put on the best version of themselves to avoid getting in trouble. When it is perfectly clear that the sheriff's in town, we are more apt to change our behavior. Even if we do this in a spiritual sense, we are still far away from truly loving God. This is something poor sinners cannot do on their own, no matter how obvious the presence of God is.

THE FATHER IN MERCY WON'T LET US OFF THE HOOK

Precisely because we think too highly of ourselves, the Lord will not cater to our whims and demands. Nevertheless, he shows all people enough to say, "You *will* know that I am real so that even if you suppress the truth to deny

---

9. Strobel, *Case for Faith*, 32.
10. Bloom was my science and faith professor in the Christian apologetics program at Biola University, La Mirada, ca. 1999–2002.

me, there will be no (real) denying me." In this way, God grants the ability for all people to know that off-ness and through it, seek God.[11]

But how does God show us just enough of himself that we might realize we need him? In two basic ways. These are known as "natural revelation," in which God gives all people just enough "natural knowledge" to realize that he is the God who is there.[12] The first way of natural revelation is in accord with Rom 1. God explains why those who suppress the truth about him have no excuse:

> For the wrath of God is revealed from heaven against all ungodliness and unrighteousness of men, who by their unrighteousness suppress the truth. For what can be known about God is plain to them, because God has shown it to them. For his invisible attributes, namely, his eternal power and divine nature, have been clearly perceived, ever since the creation of the world, in the things that have been made. So they are without excuse. (Rom 1:18–20)

And that wrath is present-day wrath when people who insist on denying and ignoring God are permitted—by his mercy—to suffer the consequences for their suppression of the truth about God. This is so that they might snap out of their self-deception and seek him.

The second basic natural revelation of God, leading to natural knowledge of God in all people is presented in Rom 2:

> For when Gentiles, who do not have the law, by nature do what the law requires, they are a law to themselves, even though they do have the law. They show that the work of the law is written on their hearts, while their conscience also bears witness, and their conflicting thoughts accuse or even excuse them. (Rom 2:14–15)

"Gentiles" are non-Jews. That is, they were not among the chosen nation of Israel that received God's law and instruction from Moses.

---

11. This is exactly the desire of God. Thus, he says, "I have no pleasure in the death of the wicked, but that the wicked turn from his way and live" (Ezek 33:11). And the word of God states, "The Lord is not slow to fulfill his promise as some count slowness, but is patient toward you, not wishing that any should perish, but that all should reach repentance" (2 Pet 3:9).

12. Natural revelations from God leading to natural knowledge of God is indeed given to all people, but these can do nothing to bring people to saving faith and salvation. For salvation, people need special revelation and special knowledge. We shall consider these later in this volume. As for my wording, the "God who is there," this is in honor of the great Christian apologist Francis Shaeffer, whose many books include a book with this same title.

Nevertheless, these non-Jews still had another law from God "written on their hearts." In fact, this is true for *all* people. This is God's gift to human beings called "conscience."

Regardless of what a person decides to do, separate from choice and action, there is something else, something separate from the thought, the decision, and the action. There is a conscience, a basic God-given knowledge that some things are right and other things are wrong, that some things are good and other things are evil. When people follow their conscience in doing the "right thing," their consciences are soothed, and they are "excused." But when people do the "wrong thing" their consciences "accuse." These wrong things are done constantly in a myriad of ways in thought, word, and deed, both by commission as well as omission.

If they are accused by their conscience, then we should thank God because their conscience is still doing its job that they might know the offness of their lives to seek God.

Over the centuries, there have been many "arguments" used to demonstrate evidence for these forms of natural revelation leading to the natural knowledge of God. What Christians must realize, however, is that the Father will not permit these to lead to saving faith. Mere knowledge is not faith, nor does it count for love. But if such knowledge heightens the awareness that something more is needed in life, then the Father will most certainly allow it for the sake of getting the attention of people who might be trying too hard to deny the living God.

CHAPTER 3 DISCUSSION GUIDE: CONTENDING FOR THE FATHER

UNCOVER INFORMATION

1. Why is it easy for a person to ask, "Where is God?"
2. According to 1 Tim 1:12–17, why did Saint Paul receive the mercy of God?
3. What was David Hume's argument against God?
4. What has God done about evil?
5. What are the two natural revelations from God given to all people so that all would know God is there?

DISCOVER MEANING

1. According to 2 Thess 2:10–12, why does God send a "strong delusion" to some people?

2. What assumption does "the problem of evil" argument make?

3. How does Job 2:10 put evil in perspective?

4. What did Jesus experience while dying on the cross that assures us that he relates when we are tempted to ask, "Where is God?"

5. What comforting promise has the Father made to his people, and why should we believe him?

EXPLORE IMPLICATIONS

1. What should the feeling of being so small do to us when we come to know the love of God?

2. Why do you think Saint Paul recorded his sordid past before his conversion?

3. Since we are aware of the conditions characterizing our world and culture during the last days, how should Christians live?

4. How does understanding Jesus' "only begotten" relationship to the Father increase our understanding of John 3:16?

5. How does the bear in the trap story help us explain the limitations of our perspective when it comes to suffering and pain?

4

Contending for the Creator

"I believe in God, the Father Almighty, **Maker** of heaven and earth."

THE FATHER'S PURPOSE IN CREATING ALL THINGS

The heavenly Father does not need to show his credentials for humanity to believe in him and to trust in him. And again, even if these were lucidly manifest, people would come back with an excuse not to believe. Nevertheless, it is to the glory of the Father that there are so many signs pointing to him. In this way—even if he has determined that these signs will lead no one to saving faith—the signs still testify to the truth that God is the Creator God.[1]

Some might say that God revealing that he has created all things is an occasion for a warped self-aggrandizement. They may say that God is promoting himself, after the manner of self-serving "gods" of Greek mythology. The Father, however, created all things not for selfish reasons, *but for us*.

As the God who *is* love, the Father created all things out of great love for us. The impetus of creation itself is a one-way gift: from God to us. God creates because he loves to give life. And while sin coming into the world

---

1. The Father reserves something else to be the revelation for saving faith for people. This honor he reserves for his only Son, Jesus Christ. This we will consider later in this volume.

corrupted life by bringing death, the Father of life and love has a made a way for life to overcome our death.[2]

THE "WAGER" OF GOD'S EXISTENCE

French philosopher, mathematician, and physicist Blaise Pascal (1623–1662) offered his famous *wager*. It is simplistic, but it provides pause for considering why investigating the natural revelation of God is worthwhile.

Pascal compared belief and unbelief in the existence of God by considering the potential gains and losses represented by that belief. He held that if one held to faith in God during their lifetime, one of these options would ensue:

1. If God did not exist, then the believer would suffer only finite loss.
2. But if God *did* exist, then the believer would experience *infinite gain*.

Pascal also leads us to also consider the other side of the wager. What if people choose to reject belief in God's existence during their lifetime? Then one of these would ensue:

1. If God did not exist, then the unbeliever was right and would suffer only finite loss.
2. But if God *did* exist, then the unbeliever would be left with *infinite loss*.

Both second possibilities of the wager about the truth of God's existence make it painfully clear what the wise position is. It would be infinitely better to have infinite gain over suffering infinite loss.

Pascal's wager, however, does not necessarily argue for believing in the Christian faith. However, if one considers the additional incentives, the allurement to his wager is even more compelling. To believe in this One is not simply to believe in an omnipotent God, but in the gracious Father who nevertheless permits us to see universal indications that he is real.

THE FATHER NOT "PROVEN," BUT RESONATING

It is wrongheaded for a Christian to assume that they have the responsibility—much less the ability—for trying to prove that God is real. No one

---

2. We shall elaborate when we get to the second article of the creed.

does. If God is God, then he is quite capable of leading anyone to know him and trust in him on his own.

Furthermore, even to assume that it is possible to "prove" God, leading to faith, is antithetical to faith itself. God himself has established the standard of faith for knowing him. Thus, God does not and will not rely on human reason to convince anyone.

At the same time, since God is God, it should not surprise us that his existence is not antithetical to what is observed in the cosmos he created. To the contrary, one should expect that what is known about the universe demonstrates complementarity with its Creator. That is, observation and reason do not contradict faith in God.

Alister McGrath explains the right approach for considering what is observable about the world and cosmos while reasonably expecting that these observations would align with the God who is there: "One cannot therefore speak meaningfully of natural theology 'proving' God's existence; it is, however, entirely appropriate to speak of a 'resonance' between theory and observation, in which it is confirmed that the fundamental themes of the Christian faith offer the best explanation of what is seen."[3] For example, God's word teaches that his creation is an extension of his love toward humanity. This creation, therefore, should demonstrate conditions which promote and preserve life. And this—in accord with all reasonable observation—is exactly what we detect. It is not surprising then that the resonance McGrath posits is consistent with what others have argued about design in the universe.

William Paley, in his *Natural Theology* (1802), argued that design in the observable order (such as the design in the human eye) is evidence of a Designer/God. The rebuttal was that perceived designed is only observed and inferred, but not at all—necessarily—innate in the thing observed.

McGrath explains, however, that "design is not an empirical datum, but reflects the interpretation of what is observed."[4] In other words, Christians may offer design not as reason to believe, but what one would expect to recognize if the things of God's word are true. He also points out that it was John Henry Newman who said, "I believe in design because I believe in God; not in God because I see design."[5]

---

3. McGrath, *Fine-Tuned Universe*, 20.
4. McGrath, *Fine-Tuned Universe*, 30.
5. McGrath, *Fine-Tuned Universe*, 30.

"Newman rightly saw that the idea of design was not 'given' within the realm of nature, but was acquired by observing and interpreting nature through the inhabitation of the Christian vision of reality."[6]

That is, the Christian faith is not a project for proving that God exists, but it is entirely a consistent logical and cohesive view of the universe. McGrath chose a good word to describe this relationship between God and the cosmos: they *resonate* which is another way of saying that the teaching of God's word and observation are consistent or are in tune with one another.

A magnificently designed cosmos is consistent with God the Father who created the universe for defined purposes: for life to be extended and for his love to be known.

CAUSATION RESONATES WITH THE FATHER

I enjoy interviews for radio and podcasts. Many years ago, one of my first interviews was regarding a published Bible study I had the privilege to write on creation.[7] On this occasion, there was the opportunity for listeners to phone in questions. I suppose the question was inevitable, and here it was: "If all things are created, then who or what created God?"

Not surprisingly, Saint Augustine had responded to this a long time before. Anything that has a *beginning* implies the existence of time. Otherwise the concept of *beginning* is nonsense.

McGrath states, "Time must therefore be thought of as one of God's creatures and servants. Augustine thus answers the question 'What was God doing before he created the universe?' by pointing out that there is no temporal 'before' in relation to the creation of the universe. God does not exist *in* time, which is a characteristic feature of the created order."[8]

In other words, the answer to the radio podcast question is, "Since God is not inside the created order (which he created), neither is he subject to time also within the created order. Furthermore, only those things which exist in time have a beginning, but since God does not exist within time which he created, he is not created."[9] J. P. Moreland explains,

---

6. McGrath, *Fine-Tuned Universe*, 30.
7. Espinosa, "Creation."
8. McGrath, *Fine-Tuned Universe*, 100.
9. Here we avoid a logical fallacy called "category mistake." Since God is outside of time and since only those things which begin existing within time are created, then God is not within the category of those things created. To assume God is confined to time

> Since the universe began to exist, it would seem that the most reasonable view to take would be that the first event was caused. The principle that something does not come from nothing without a cause is a reasonable one. This is especially true with regard to events. Events have a definite beginning and end, and do not happen without something causing them. By contrast, God does not need a cause, since he is neither an event nor a contingent being. He is a necessary Being and such a being doesn't need a cause. In fact, it is a category fallacy to ask for a cause for God since this is really asking for a cause for an uncaused being.[10]

The Christian worldview, however, maintains that *everything else*, other than God, was created. And this idea is not unreasonable, nor is it unintelligent. It also resonates with a legitimate way to view what is real and exists in time and space.

The great contemporary apologist and philosopher William Lane Craig is compelling in his presentation of the *kalam* (which means "argument"), which is the cosmological argument for the existence of God. Again, it is not offered as "proof" but as an example of resonance with the God who is already there.

> Premise 1: Whatever begins to exist has a cause.
> Premise 2: The universe began to exist.
> Conclusion: Therefore, the universe has a cause.[11]

William Lane Craig himself points out that the most challenging part of the syllogism[12] is premise 2 but then goes on to defend it through both scientific observations and philosophical analyses. After presenting a host of scientific observations consistent with the inflationary theory[13] of the universe pointing to the universe having a beginning, he goes on to some important philosophical considerations.[14]

---

mismatches the categories of eternity (surpassing time) with being confined to time.

10. Moreland, *Scaling the Secular City*, 38.

11. Geivett, "*Kalam* Cosmological Argument," 62.

12. A syllogism consists of two premises (major and minor) and a logical conclusion.

13. That is, the traditional theory of how the universe expands from a single point of unleashed energy, sometimes referred to as "the big bang," though from the perspective of creation, it would not entail anything random.

14. I have mentioned above that no matter what arguments are put forth, there is typically, an "out clause" returned as volley. In this case, the Christian apologist will be prepared for alternative models of the universe, including the oscillating model or—and what is more popular currently—the multiverse model.

One of those considerations seems straightforward: the idea of a universe that is infinite with no beginning and no end would represent an actual infinite. And an actual infinite, which is a series of events with no beginning, cannot exist.

This observation does not apply to theoretical or mathematical infinites. Certainly, mathematical infinites exist within the realm of mathematics. For example, the number of points in infinite space can be the same number of points on a twelve-inch ruler. In this sense, even an inch on a ruler may contain as many points as all the light years in the entire universe, or even multiple universes, if they existed.[15]

But somehow, we know intuitively that this comparison falls short of what is actual and real (even while mathematics remains coherently true). Again J. P. Moreland elucidates,

> A beginningless universe has no first member. Before any event in the history of the cosmos, there are already transpired an actual infinite number of events. So no matter how far back one goes in one's mind, one is no closer to traversing the past than before he began counting—even if he counts back through an infinite number of events (which is impossible). In light of such a beginningless infinite series, neither the present, nor tomorrow, nor *any* moment in the past could be reached.[16]

But what is undeniably evident is that we have indeed arrived at the present; therefore, the universe is not an actual infinite. It had a beginning, and if it had beginning, it had a cause. And therefore,

> in summary, it is most reasonable to believe that the universe had a beginning which was caused by a timeless, immutable agent. This is not a proof that such a being is the God of the Bible, but it is a strong statement that the world had its beginning by the act of a person. And this is at the very least a good reason to believe in some form of theism.[17]

The Apostles' Creed, however, does more than confess mere theism (that a personal God exists), but goes further to help us to know what Luther said, "He does [all this] out of fatherly, divine goodness and mercy,

---

15. Moreland, *Scaling the Secular City*, 21.
16. Moreland, *Scaling the Secular City*, 29–30.
17. Moreland, *Scaling the Secular City*, 42.

without any merit or worthiness in me."[18] And what is "all this" at this juncture? It is the cause of all things to come into existence, including our lives. For this alone it is our "duty to thank and praise, serve and obey Him. This is most certainly true."[19]

DESIGN RESONATES WITH THE FATHER

Once again, God does not need people to notice signs of his presence for him to be. Nevertheless, one of these signs is the design of all that exists. He permits design to be evident even to the extent that it undeniably points to the Designer, God himself. Thus, the Holy Scriptures put forth the truth that "his invisible attributes, namely, his eternal power and divine nature, have been clearly perceived, ever since the creation of the world, in the things that have been made" (Rom 1:20).

Stephen C. Meyer might be the leading Christian apologist of our time regarding the complexity of the cell as entirely consistent with the existence of God. And from this single, minute example of what is in the world, he makes the powerful case that "there is simply too much information in the cell to be explained by chance alone."[20]

He explains that "chance . . . cannot explain the origin of information through natural selection acting on random changes."[21] And DNA is the grand example of this seemingly irrefutable observation. DNA's information implies intentional programming that eliminates the possibly that the information is accidental. Again, there is just too much information in DNA to be attributed to chance. "Saying otherwise," says Meyer, "is like saying a newspaper headline might arise from the chemical attraction between ink and paper."[22] Living cells and the information latent within these cells, however, is evidence of real design.

Meyer, however, also points out that living cells are not the only evidence of design in the created order. Design is evident not only when it comes to what is within us but also appears in the cosmos around us. This design is often referred to as the "fine-tuning" of the universe when and where a multitude of factors in the universe converge for life to exist such as gravity,

---

18. Luther, *Small Catechism*, 16.
19. Luther, *Small Catechism*, 16.
20. Meyer, "What Is the Evidence," 145.
21. Meyer, "What Is the Evidence," 145.
22. Meyer, "What Is the Evidence," 145.

electromagnetic energy, the earth's placement in relation to the sun, and our solar system's location within the Milky Way galaxy. Meyer elaborates,

> Many physicists have noted that this fine-tuning strongly suggests design by a pre-existent intelligence. Physicist Paul Davies has said that "the impression of design is overwhelming." Fred Hoyle argued, "A commonsense interpretation of the facts suggests that a superintellect has monkeyed with physics, as well as chemistry and biology." Many physicists now concur. They would argue that—in effect—these parameters appear finely tuned to make life possible because some*one* carefully fine-tuned them.[23]

That "fined-tuned" condition of the universe for people is known as "the anthropic principle." Hugh Ross states, "The uniformity, homogeneity, size, and mass and dark energy densities of the universe must all be precisely as they are for human life to be possible."[24] Ross also presents a staggering list of requirements for a "just right" universe that would be necessary for the existence of human life on earth. He elaborates,

> To put this situation in perspective, imagine the possibility of a Boeing 747 aircraft being completely assembled as a result of a tornado striking a junkyard. Now imagine how much more unlikely that possibility would be if [something else] is substituted for the junk parts.... So, too, as one examines the building blocks necessary for life to come into existence, the possibility of that happening without someone or something designing them stretches the imagination beyond the breaking point.[25]

But the "just right" conditions for human life to be possible do not only apply to the universe around us, but also to the planet we inhabit. Ross explains,

> For life molecules to operate so that organisms can live requires an environment where water vapor, liquid water, and frozen water are all stable and abundant. This means that a planet cannot be too close to its star or too far away. In the case of planet Earth, given a particular atmosphere, a change in the distance from the sun as small as 2% would rid the planet of all life.[26]

---

23. Meyer, "What Is the Evidence," 147.
24. Ross, *Creator and the Cosmos*, 138.
25. Ross, *Creator and the Cosmos*, 167.
26. Ross, *Creator and the Cosmos*, 208–9.

As if the breathtaking exactness of what is required of the universe and our planet for human life to exist were not enough, there is another astonishing feature we ought not take for granted: we can observe the universe as if looking through a glorious window through which we can view God's miraculous handiwork. Hugh Ross states, "We are granted an unobstructed view—in a language understandable to all—of God's glory, power, and righteousness written in the heavens."[27] And this of course is exactly what God's word proclaims: "The heavens declare the glory of God, and the sky proclaims his handiwork" (Ps 19:1).

In light of these astounding truths of fine-tuning, cosmologist Edward Harrison advances, "Here is the . . . design argument of Paley—updated and refurbished. . . . Take your choice: blind chance that requires multitudes of universes or design that requires only one."[28]

MORALITY RESONATES WITH THE FATHER

Morality exists. Depending on which worldview one might consult, the reasons for their existence will vary considerably. However, there is an interesting thing to take note of: if any of those reasons are from a nontheistic worldview (no personal God), then all of them hover between total meaninglessness of values as something purely imagined, on the one hand, to what people must assign to morals for morals to have meaning, on the other.

It is only the theistic view that assigns morals to the nature of God himself.[29] The moral argument for the existence of God may be presented this way:

---

27. Ross, *Creator and the Cosmos*, 206–7.

28. Ross, *Creator and the Cosmos*, 179–80. William Paley (1743–1805), English theologian and philosopher, put forth a design argument for God's existence, especially remembered for his "watch" illustration: if one found a watch in an open field, one would rightly conclude it had a maker. Likewise, Paley argued, to examine the world, is to also conclude a Designer.

29. Thus, here the famous *Euthyphro* dilemma is answered. God neither assigns meaning and value to life (and its morality) in an arbitrary manner *nor* do meaning and value in life (and its morality) independently exist apart from God. This, however, is an either-or fallacy. The other option, and the one consistent with a theistic worldview, is that people bear the marks of meaning and value intrinsically because they were created in the image of God, which demonstrates that God's nature itself grants meaning and value. Good morals are therefore an extension of the nature of God.

> Premise 1: If objective moral values exist, then God exists.
> Premise 2: Objective moral values do exist.
> Conclusion: Therefore, God exists.[30]

Neo-Darwinism, naturalism, and philosophical materialism would, however, classify morality as imagined or generated simply for the preservation of the species. If this were the case, *why would morals be important or necessary?*

Even *preservation* of the species implies some kind of inherent value in people, but there is no reason to assign such value to humanity in these systems. Value in such a context would be completely arbitrary because people in such a view are like animals, and animals just do what animals do. No one questions an animal killing another animal. Such killings are simply an example of survival of the fittest. Morality in this view is a nonfactor and the height of social construct.

There is simply no good reason that can be given for morals apart from God. If nature and matter is all that exists and people are without eternal souls, then any reason given is without any coherent value. There is no reason at the end of the day to honor and uphold meaningful morality. But if God exists, then morality itself is actual because God's nature—the basis and source of all morality—is also actual.

Paul Copan presents the phenomena we observe in the universe in a column alongside two other columns. One column represents a theistic context, that God is real. The other column represents a naturalistic context. In every instance, the phenomena either have rich meaning in relation to the theistic context or to the naturalistic context rendering the phenomena as arbitrary and (if naturalism were true) irrelevant and insignificant. In other words, if God is real, then many assumptions about morals are meaningful, but if God is not real, then these observations are meaningless and without value. This means that any "value" assigned would be imagined by the observer. A theistic view, however, affirms

- humans have self-consciousness;
- personal beings exist;
- humans make free personal decisions and choices;
- our senses and rational faculties are generally reliable in producing true beliefs;

30. Copan, "Moral Argument," 109.

- human beings have intrinsic value/dignity and rights;
- objective moral values exist;
- beauty exists (e.g., not only in landscapes and sunsets but in "elegant" or "beautiful" scientific theories); and
- the universe is finely tuned for human life (known as "the Goldilocks effect"—the universe is "just right" for life).[31]

That is, the heavenly Father in every phenomenon listed above fills our lives with real meaning and thus, for every person reading this, assures each reader that they too have meaning and value. One is wise to consider the revelation of God pointing ultimately to the heavenly Father. In and through him every phenomenon listed is a gift that we might know his love.

If, on the other hand, the phenomenon listed are viewed as accidental characteristics of naturalism, then it is small wonder why so many resist God. But if they do so, they do it not because anyone has proven that God is not real but because it suits them to live for themselves and be their own authority.

And this one self-serving reality is the reason we must contend for the faith, but there are some things in the culture that fully take advantage of the naturalistic view.

WHEN THE CULTURE STANDS AGAINST THE FATHER

While AI has been with us in rudimentary forms for over a century, its exponential growth is undeniable. While much good can come from AI, it also typifies how core sin might consider another opportunity for a tower of Babel, which in Scripture (Gen 11) was mankind's expression of self-aggrandizement and rebellion against God. Saint Paul extends wisdom to all who would pay attention: "All things are lawful for me [including AI], but I will not be dominated by anything" (1 Cor 6:12). In other words, we must always keep God first in our lives, not becoming dependent on any human invention to save us.

How will we proceed? As we ponder that question, there is little doubt that we need to contend for the faith once delivered by contending in the culture against two natural tendencies that will come out as AI continues to expand.

---

31. Copan, "Moral Argument," 114.

1. The inward tendency: More than ever before, virtual worlds will be made available to people. There will be vastly more reasons and conveniences for self-isolation. Self-isolation will lead to the further decline of the church, which inherently relies upon communities of people gathering, and self-isolation will insulate people from living out the greatest mandates of the faith to serve others in love and to witness to the gospel for those who do not know Jesus Christ.

2. The outward tendency: More than ever before, people will be tempted to think that anything we could possibly need in our day-to-day lives will be supplied through the technology offered by AI. The more we experience AI and its corollary of biotechnology, the more people will be tempted to think that all needs will be covered by an outer source that is not God.

It is important to point out that none of this implies that AI is inherently evil. It's not. That would be like saying a smartphone or laptop computer is evil. The question is how sin, the world, and the devil will try to manipulate whatever culture presents to us.

One example converges with our prior discussion on stage two "I" and the current one on "Father." If anyone abides in the second stage "I," then they will be more apt to think in the face of advanced AI that their off-ness can be solved through AI. In time, there will be more options through AI to address whatever we do not like about who and what we are. Sin will lead people to consider integrating with biotechnology for increased expressions of new categories which go beyond male and female, and while these will seem exciting at first, we will most likely completely underestimate further corruption of the self.

In terms of relationships, people driven by sin are driving a perversion that is already seen in manufacturers and inventors trying to make AI a source of "companionship" in ways that enter the realm of sexual immorality. The knee-jerk response will be—as is often said in the face of sin—"But the user is not hurting anybody."

The truth, however, is that not only is the user or customer hurting themselves, but they are contributing to a trend that will not only increase loneliness but will make it even more difficult for societies to form meaningful human relationships.

This is exactly why Christians must contend for the faith once delivered. Not only are we to always uphold the most important companionship between a man and a woman in holy marriage, but also to live as the community of God in the church and in extended communities in the culture that treat other people as loved by the Father.

There are some things, therefore, that the church must contend with in the culture as children of God who know the Father:

1. We cannot place our hope in anything over and above God the Father.
2. We cannot permit anything to define our lives other than God the Father.
3. We cannot permit anything to be treated as the cause or source (or preserver) of our lives other than God the Father.
4. We cannot treat anything as the source of order and beauty other than God the Father.
5. We cannot permit anything other than God the Father to dictate right morals and values.
6. We cannot allow for isolationism to take over by failing to foster community under the care of God the Father.
7. We cannot permit to entrust our health and peace to any outward resource in the place of God the Father.

But what will motivate people to be vigilant in such contending? Only one thing—rather, only One person, the Lord Jesus Christ. To the second article of the Apostles' Creed we now turn.

CHAPTER 4 DISCUSSION GUIDE: CONTENDING FOR THE CREATOR

UNCOVER INFORMATION

1. Why did God create all things?
2. What is Pascal's wager?
3. Why should the Christian avoid trying to "prove" God's existence?
4. How do we answer the question, "Who created God?"
5. What evidence for design (and therefore a Designer) exists?

DISCOVER MEANING

1. What is the *kalam* cosmological argument for the existence of God?
2. Why is an actual infinite seemingly impossible?
3. What is the "anthropic principle," and how does this make the existence of a Designer more compelling?
4. What is the moral argument for the existence of God?
5. What is the potential danger in advanced AI, and how should Christians respond?

EXPLORE IMPLICATIONS

1. If there is even a chance that unbelief could lead to infinite loss, what should people do?
2. If design is only imagined and not real, what are the implications for life's meaning?
3. If morality is only a human construct, what are the implications for "good" and "evil"?
4. How should Christians counter both the inward and outward tendencies of AI?
5. Regarding the seven imperatives about remaining faithful to God the Father, what would happen to culture if these convictions are lost?

PART II

Contending for the Faith According to the Second Article of the Creed

5

Contending for Jesus Christ of Real History

"I believe in God, . . . and in Jesus Christ, his only Son, our Lord, who was *conceived* by the Holy Spirit, *born* of the Virgin Mary; *suffered* under Pontius Pilate . . ."

IN TIME CAME THE GODMAN

The Holy Scriptures refer to the coming of the Lord Jesus Christ into human history this way: "But when the fullness of time had come, God sent forth his Son" (Gal 4:4). And when that fullness came, the incarnation occurred.

The incarnation of Jesus Christ is reflected in John 1, verses 1 and 14: "In the beginning was the Word, and the Word was with God, and the Word was God. . . . And the Word became flesh and dwelt among us, and we have seen his glory, glory as of the only Son from the Father, full of grace and truth."

The incarnation is God taking on flesh. It points to Jesus, who is the eternal second person of the Holy Trinity, voluntarily becoming enfleshed. In this instance, God and man was in one person: Jesus Christ. This is the indispensable article of faith called "the incarnation."

It is hard to describe the enormous importance of the incarnation[1] to the Christian faith. What makes or breaks the Christian faith is the teaching

---

1. God taking on flesh is what is meant by the "incarnation." It is not to be confused

that Jesus Christ was—and still is, by the way—God in the flesh (by the incarnation). Apart from that one fact, every other teaching of Christianity is, for all intents and purposes, void and meaningless. It has been said that the most important teaching of the saving faith is that we are saved by grace through faith in Christ apart from the works of the law. However, if the true teaching of Jesus' incarnation is compromised, then the gospel comes falling like a house of cards.

It is for this reason that so-called "progressive" versions which compromise the true divinity of Jesus are sad and dying replicas of the original saving faith. Furthermore, they have no power to save people and are bankrupt in religious teachings.

Luther further described the importance of the incarnation: "There is no other God than this Man Jesus Christ."[2] Furthermore, the Reformer asserted the faith of the early church: "Christ is not a mere man but is true God and man at the same time."[3] In addition, Luther elucidated, "The Person is made up of the divine and the human nature. . . . Therefore Christ is true God and true man."[4] These basic truths demonstrate the axiom "remove the divinity of Christ and lose salvation altogether":

> Here you see how necessary it is to believe and confess the doctrine of the divinity of Christ. When Arius denied this, it was necessary also for him to deny the doctrine of the redemption. For to conquer the sin of the world, death, the curse, and the wrath of God in Himself—this is the work, not of any creature but of the divine power. Therefore it was necessary that He who was to conquer these in Himself should be true God by nature. For in opposition to this mighty power—sin, death, and the curse—which of itself reigns in the whole world and in the entire creation, it is necessary to set an even higher power, which cannot be found and does not exist apart from the divine power. . . . Hence those who deny the divinity of Christ lose all Christianity.[5]

---

with similar sounding religious teachings like "reincarnation," which is the idea of the transmigration of the human soul, from Eastern religions, nor is it to be confused with "immaculate conception," which is a Roman Catholic teaching regarding the Virgin Mary. Rather, the "incarnation" is reflected in John 1:1 and 14, as quoted above.

2. Luther, *Galatians*, 29.
3. Luther, *Galatians*, 62.
4. Luther, *Galatians*, 367.
5. Luther, *Galatians*, 283.

With these words, it is clear that Luther understood what was at stake. By itself, Christ's humanity could not conquer sin and death, but on account of the divinity, Christ had all power with the ability to accomplish exactly that. And yet, at the same time, without his humanity he could not do it vicariously. He could not have done it as our substitute, representing all humanity. Both natures were necessary for us to be rescued from all that threatens our lives.

Without his human nature, he could not be *our* Savior from sin and death, and without his divine nature, he could not have had the power necessary to accomplish that salvation along with the authority to do it for all people. But Jesus Christ had both; therefore, all who trust in him have the forgiveness of sins and eternal life. This One, this Jesus for us, is the reason there is life beyond death and why our bodies wracked by sin will be resurrected through the victory Christ won for us.

WOULDN'T THIS BE NICE IF . . .

You might know the saying we've started in the subtitle; can you finish it? The rest is ". . . it were true." Some people evoke this saying because the good news of Jesus Christ sounds too good to be true. But why not believe it? There are two basic reasons why some doubt Jesus Christ being God in the flesh and able to save all people from sin and death:

1. The incarnation enters the realm of the miraculous
2. The life of Christ is not understood as real history

When these two basic reasons for skepticism are given, it is easy to hone in on what needs to be addressed. First, let's appreciate the word "miracle." In the word of God, it is not some deep, dark mysterious thing. In the New Testament Greek, the word is *sēmeion*. That is, the word means "sign." And in the case of Jesus Christ, it means he did things or gave signs—when combined with his testimony about himself—which pointed to his divinity.

MIRACLE/SIGN: NOT A BAD WORD

There are two ways to go about discussing miracles and signs. One way is to begin with the miracle of Christ's resurrection from the dead, but we will save this for chapter 7. The other way is to begin our approach to discuss miracles, not with what occurs on earth but what is beyond earth and, for that matter, beyond the universe. But first, let us clarify what a miracle *is not*.

One of the most popular ways of defining a miracle is to say, "A miracle is a violation of the laws of nature." Why go there? If someone were to drop an apple from my study on the second floor of my house, anyone observing this would observe the effects of gravity in all its grandeur. The apple doesn't have a chance. The law of gravity says it *must* fall.

But if I stand in my driveway underneath the window from where the apple was dropped, and I stretched out my hand to catch the apple, this, then, is anything but a violation of the laws of nature. My catching would not have violated anything that would normally occur in the natural course of things. All my catching would do is introduce an *intervention* of another power *interacting* with the original event: in this case a *suspension* of the falling apple. No violations of the laws of nature here at all.

To extend the analogy above in application to a miracle is to say that since God is real, he has the prerogative to be the One to catch the apple, and if he did—again—no violation of the laws of nature would occur. *What would be different, though, is that we cannot observe the intervention and interaction as we could observe me doing the same thing.*

Richard Purtill points out, "As an event caused by divine will acting from outside this natural order, a miracle neither confirms nor disconfirms any generalization about the natural order of things."[6]

But why would the Christian faith consider God catching that apple a possibility? The first of two ways for discussing miracles is to take a "top-down" approach.[7] The approach is not at all complicated and is extraordinarily logical.

The top-down approach argues that miracles are possible because God exists beyond (or atop) the universe, and because God is there, he can interact with what occurs within the universe. That is, here we consider two major ways of looking at our existence and understanding reality:

1. One is a closed-universe view (there is no God).
2. The other is an open-universe view (God is there).

The closed universe takes us back to naturalism that we mentioned above in chapter 4. Naturalism asserts that all that exists and all that is real is

---

6. Purtill, "Defining Miracles," 69.
7. The concept was introduced to me by one of my professors at Biola University, La Mirada, Douglas Geivett, ca. 1999–2002.

physical and materialistic. Therefore, there is nothing outside the universe. The universe is both eternal and represents all reality. Of course, the moment one asserts this position, there is an automatic hint at an impressive faith in something that—like creation—cannot be reproduced in a scientific laboratory. There is no way to "prove" one or the other position. Both positions require some kind of faith.

The famous atheistic philosopher David Hume would object to my conclusion. From his point of view, he was being quite objective about the whole matter. His argument against miracles may be presented as follows.

> Premise 1: A miracle is a violation of the laws of nature.
> Premise 2: We have uniform experience that the laws of nature are never violated.
> Conclusion: Therefore, miracles cannot occur.

Unfortunately for Hume, however, and as Flew[8] has said, "Hume is in a particularly bad position to give an argument like this. For him, 'laws of nature' are simply observed regularities that embody no necessity. . . . Thus to say that miracles violate laws of nature is simply to say that there is uniform experience against them, a return to the question-begging argument."[9]

Both the closed and open views of the universe require some faith, and both views require the belief in something that accounts for the existence of everything else. Therefore, the challenge in the discussion isn't really about the word "miracle" or "sign," but about the understanding of "laws of nature."

To the believer in God, "laws of nature" may be intelligently discussed in relation to God outside the universe, but for the naturalist, "laws of nature" never interact with anything outside of nature itself.

As a result, there is still a problem with the concept of naturalism. That mechanism for accounting for the existence of the universe only pushes back against the question. So, where did *that* come from? Both require extraordinary faith, but one thing is for certain: naturalism in no way, shape, or form disproves the possibility of miracles, especially since it cannot prove itself.

In the meantime, the open-universe model not only permits the possibility of miracles, but when put alongside the other considerations in

---

8. Anthony Flew was an English philosopher who left atheism for theism, and while he had defended David Hume, he was not afraid to point out some deficiencies.

9. Purtill, "Defining Miracles," 67. Question-begging is when an argument's premises assume the conclusion to be true.

chapter 4 above, it leads us to the importance of realizing that the miracles associated with Jesus Christ come not in the context of fairy tales but of real human history.

ONCE UPON A TIME IN REAL HUMAN HISTORY

The Holy Bible[10] is written as real history.[11] Simply put, it is about real people in real places while participating in the real events of real human history. Here is one example from Saint Luke's gospel:

> In those days a decree went out from Caesar Augustus that all the world should be registered. This was the first registration when Quirinius was governor of Syria. And all went to be registered, each to his own town. And Joseph also went up from Galilee, from the town of Nazareth, to Judea, to the city of David, which is called Bethlehem, because he was of the house and lineage of David, to be registered with Mary, his betrothed, who was with child. (Luke 2:1–5)

While such detailed sections of Holy Scripture might not qualify as the most exciting, they are extraordinarily valuable in upholding the historical integrity and reliability of God's word. The details are unafraid of inviting historical scrutiny. In Luke 2:1–5 we can examine these historical questions:

1. Which Caesar was in power during this time?
2. Was there a census conducted during his time?
3. Was Quirinius the governor of Syria at this time?
4. Was Galilee a region in northern Israel?
5. Was Nazareth a city in this region?

---

10. That is, the thirty-nine books of the Old Testament and twenty-seven books of the New Testament, with the understanding that the Roman Catholic Church also accepts as the books of the Apocrypha as canonical. If one accepts these books, then one must include another fourteen, and perhaps another three in recognition of the Eastern Orthodox tradition. The sixty-six books of God's word, however, have universal acceptance within all Christendom.

11. The Holy Bible also uses a variety of genres (unique forms of written communication) such as poetry (e.g., Psalms), apocalyptic (e.g., Ezekiel and Revelation), wisdom literature (e.g., Proverbs), etc. However, all these serve the overarching line of direction, and the vast majority of its content and books are presented in standard historical narrative, the language of recorded history.

6. Was Bethlehem a city in this region?

7. Were Joseph and Mary citizens during this time and in this place?

If one wanted to start a religion based on imaginative fabrications, then assuredly, the handbook for lies and fairy tales would recommend, "Do *not* make mention of real times, places, events, and people!" But why not? Because then one would invite skeptics to check the details of the story. The moment that is done, it would be easy to find out that it's fake.

On the other hand, if one desired to give a truthful account of what actually occurred in human history, then these are the sorts of details that would be attributed to accurate historical records and would be expected by the scrupulous reader aware that the Scriptures tell of the Savior of the world. If such is the revelation, then details matter.

F. F. Bruce expands on the details of Luke 2:1–5:

> Josephus informs us that towards the end of Herod's reign (37–34 BC) the Emperor Augustus treated him more as a subject than as a friend, and that all Judaea took an oath of allegiance to Augustus as well as to Herod. The holding of an imperial census in a client kingdom (as Judaea was during Herod's reign) is not unparalleled; in the reign of Tiberius a census was imposed on the client kingdom of Antiochus in eastern Asia Minor. [Furthermore] the obligation on all persons to be enrolled at their domiciles of origin, which made it necessary for Joseph to return to Bethlehem, has been illustrated from an edict of AD 104, in which C. Vibius Maximus, Roman prefect of Egypt, gives notice. . . . [Moreover] there is scattered evidence of the holding of enrolments in various parts of the Empire between 11 and 8 BC, the papyrus evidence in the case of Egypt being practically conclusive.[12]

But what of Quirinius? Naysayers have had a field day with Quirinius. We know from history who the governors of Syria were, and at the time of the birth of Christ, Quirinius was not the governor (though he would eventually be by the time he is referred to in Acts 5:37, during the census of AD 6). However, this is exactly the sort of thing one should expect to encounter in piecing history together.

Arthur Just clues us in, however, on an important detail: "One simple grammatical solution to the problem of the census in Luke is to understand πρώτη [typically translated 'when'] as adverbial and as governing this

---

12. Bruce, *New Testament Documents*, 87.

genitive participle phrase: 'before Quirinius governed Syria.'"[13] Just cites M.-J. Lagrange, who points out that the registration of Quirinius mentioned in Acts 5:37 was *the* registration which marked the annexation of Judea.[14] It thus provided a historical marker for the historical context of a lesser census.

But such is the stuff of real history. It is taking in hand the things that are real and actual, and then knowing that one can sort them out *precisely because they occurred in history.*

And such is the overall quality of the Holy Bible. Christian apologist Ron Rhodes has exquisitely detailed the historical and nonmythological character of Sacred Scripture.[15] Below are several of the attributes of the Holy Bible:

1. Genealogies: Gen 5, 10, 11; 1 Chr 1–9; Matt 1; Luke 1
2. Inclusion of geographical notes: Gen 13:10, Deut 1:1–2
3. Presence of chronological notes: Luke 3:1–2, Gal 1:18, 2:1
4. Bibliographical notes: 1 Kgs 24:5, Luke 1:1–3
5. Explicit factual claims: John 21:24; Acts 2:32 ("we all are witnesses"), 26:25–26
6. Explicit denial of myth: 2 Tim 4:3–4, 2 Pet 1:16, and 1 John 1:1–3 presenting empirical evidence
7. Claims of eyewitness testimony: Luke 1:2, 1 Cor 15:6, 1 John 1:1
8. Statements that the readers knew to be true: Gal 1:13
9. Unflattering stories: Peter's denial of Christ; the women at the tomb before the apostles; King David's failures; Christ's brothers who did not believe in him; and, from the world's perspective, even the passion and cross of Jesus Christ
10. Statements that base faith on historical events: 1 Cor 15, Ps 105

---

13. Just, *Luke*, 103.
14. Just, *Luke*, 104.
15. As he did for me while he was one of my professors at Biola University, ca. 2000–2002.

THE SCRIPTURES RING TRUE

Point number 9 above is one of my personal favorites. Again, let's consider the hypothetical con artist of religion. If he or she were trying to start a new religion and wanted to do his or her very best to convince people that it was legitimate, then the last thing he or she would present were the failures of key adherents to that religion. The Christian faith, however, is chock-full of failures associated with Christianity.

Saint Peter might be one of the stronger examples of this. Yes, he was a leader among the apostles, and yes, Scripture attributes some very impressive accomplishments of the one renamed by Jesus from "Simon" to "Peter," which means "rock." But the record of his embarrassments is substantial.

Saint Peter was skeptical towards Christ's command to throw the nets out for fish after catching nothing all night long (Luke 5:5); he was openly confused about Jesus' parable of the four soils (Matt 15:16); he, with the other disciples, misinterpreted the meaning of Christ's warning about "the yeast of the Pharisees" (Matt 16:11); Peter, with the other disciples, tried to keep the children away from Jesus as he was teaching (Mark 10:13); he sank into the water after taking his eyes off Christ (Matt 14:30); he joined the prideful debate about who was the greatest among the disciples (Mark 9:33–34, Luke 22:24); he put his foot in his mouth as he rambled, not knowing what to say during the transfiguration of Christ (Matt 17:4, Mark 9:5, Luke 9:33); he, Peter, tried to stop Jesus from accomplishing his saving work on the cross to which Jesus says to him, "Get behind me, Satan! You are a hindrance to me. For you are not setting your mind on the things of God, but on the things of man" (Matt 16:23, Mark 8:33); he tried to keep Jesus from washing his feet (John 13:8); he denied Jesus three times, as recorded in the Gospels, after Jesus was arrested and on trial (Matt 26:69–75, Mark 14:66–72, Luke 22:55–65, John 18:25–27); and after being equipped in the Spirit to be powerful in word and deed, he committed hypocrisy in broad daylight, giving occasion for Saint Paul to publicly correct him (Gal 2:11–14).

Not only are these things *not* a detriment to the integrity of the Holy Bible, but they strengthen its trustworthiness. The Holy Bible is marked by the realistic portrayal of real people in real life. Even the strongest leaders are not perfect; even the greatest ones fall short. The Holy Scriptures do not try to hide these things but put them forward precisely because these bear the marks of truth about humanity even among the greatest Christian leaders. These added details heighten the ringing of truth.

But that is not the only thing that comes out of recounting Saint Peter's downfalls. The greater witness is to what Jesus did in the face of them. Saint Peter was forgiven and restored, and his is the account of Jesus' attitude toward all human beings impacted by core sin: they are not condemned by Jesus, nor do their sins define them in the eyes of the God of grace. Instead, sinners are restored, healed, and given new lives in Christ. In spite of all his failures, this was true for Saint Peter, and it is true for all who confess the Lord Jesus Christ.

THE GOLD STANDARD OF TRUTH: FALSIFIABILITY

The last point on the list above, "Statements that base faith on historical events," might be the most important. Here, the integrity for the Christian faith does not rest upon subjective convictions but upon either what did or did not occur in human history. And what can never be taken for granted are the historical and verified circumstances surrounding the resurrection of the Lord Jesus Christ.

In 1 Corinthians, we encounter a spectacular assertion by Saint Paul: "And if Christ has not been raised, then our preaching is in vain and your faith is in vain" (1 Cor 15:14). To make sure we didn't miss the significance of his statement the first time, Saint Paul continues with this: "And if Christ has not been raised, your faith is futile, and you are still in your sins" (1 Cor 15:17). He goes on to remind the reader that if Christ in fact did not rise from death, then those who have died have simply "perished," (1 Cor 15:18) and furthermore, that if followers in Christ have hope in this life alone without Christ having conquered the grave, then "we are of all people most to be pitied" (1 Cor 15:19).

These statements are enormously significant and demonstrate one of the most telling characteristics of statements of fact and true conditions. These statements demonstrate something known as *falsifiability*.[16] Karl Popper (1902–1994), an Austrian philosopher of science, suggested

---

16. In simple terms, if one can show that a crucial aspect of any claim is false, then the entire claim must also be false. For example, if Christ did not actually rise from death, then Christianity is false. Conversely, if the resurrection of Christ cannot be disproven, then we may trust the truth claims of the Christian faith. What is crucial here, however, is that these crucial claims can be investigated. If I assert that I saw a fifteen-foot purple gorilla in the woods, my claim cannot be investigated and is therefore not falsifiable. The assertion of the historical resurrection of Jesus, however, did not happen in a corner. It can be investigated and the historical evidence has not failed the test of falsifiability.

that "falsifiability" is a more reliable criterion of both meaning and truth than is verifiability. We must seek hypotheses which are "falsifiable," which can be disproved by negative instances. Indeed, the more falsifiable the hypothesis, the more valuable it is likely to be. If negative instances are not found we begin to gain confidence in its truth.[17]

It's important to grasp the magnitude of falsifiability applied to the truth claims of Holy Scripture. The word of God continually reminds us that we do not trust in it as a source of truth and authority based upon subjective criteria. It does not encourage blind acceptance nor does it hide in the corner of untestable testimonies by religious leaders. Instead, the word of God is testable and is easily scrutinized. For example, if it records a future prediction in the Old Testament about Jesus' public ministry in the first century AD, then we may ask, "Was this prophetic prediction fulfilled or not?" The answer to the question does not rely on religious feeling, but on objective facts.

There is no litmus test based on esoteric religious experience; there is no blind insistence that you listen to an authority figure simply because they claim to know what you do not. None of these things belong to the truth-quality of the Holy Bible. When it comes to the Christian faith, all these cheap versions of why to believe are rejected and jettisoned.

Christianity openly and lucidly puts all its legitimacy *upon what has occurred in history—namely, the resurrection of the Lord Jesus Christ*. We will elaborate on the pivotal nature of the resurrection of Jesus in chapter 7, but for now, the credentials for the saving faith are clear: they rest on real history, and this, indeed, is the stuff of truth. If one were to demonstrate that the resurrection of Jesus Christ did not occur in human history, then, point blank, the Christian faith is not true. But if the resurrection of Jesus Christ stands as having occurred in human history, then the entirety of the Christian faith is reliable and trustworthy.

JESUS IN HISTORY: THANK YOU, PONTIUS PILATE

You know the saying "Guilt by association," but in this case the association the Lord Christ has with Pontius Pilate is advantageous regarding the historicity of Christ and his word. I was once asked by a parishioner, "Why must we constantly repeat this man's name whenever we confess the saving

---

17. Reese, *Dictionary*, 594.

faith?" Even though it may seem an oddity to keep mentioning this Roman procurator's name, the inference behind it is important. The reason is precisely because the Lord Jesus Christ lived, died, and was raised in real history, associated with real people living in real places while conducting their real lives. From the perspective of civilization in the first century, the record of the real Jesus Christ was further substantiated by the record of a Roman official as told by a Roman historian. This is what accurate history is made of.

Cornelius Tacitus (ca. AD 55–120) was a Roman historian, "called the 'greatest historian' of ancient Rome, an individual generally acknowledged among scholars for his moral 'integrity and essential goodness.'"[18] In his work entitled *Annals* written in AD 115, Tacitus wrote, "Christus, from whom the name [Christians] had its origin, suffered the extreme penalty during the reign of Tiberius at the hands of one of our procurators, Pontius Pilatus."[19]

That is to say, the glories of the faith listed in the Apostles' Creed are also anchored in space and time, in real history, because there can be no Savior of the world who did not actually come into the world. But he did, and Pontius Pilate, the one in charge of his execution, was there in real history to confirm it.

HISTORICAL RELIABILITY OF SCRIPTURE: IN A CLASS BY ITSELF

There are three outstanding reasons why we can know that the New Testament documents which reveal the Savior Christ are historically trustworthy. The reasons are Holy Scripture's credentials in respect to (1) bibliographical evidence, (2) internal evidence, and (3) external evidence.[20]

Bibliographical Evidence

As the name implies, bibliographical evidence has to do with the *biblio* or the "book" evidence of Holy Scripture, especially in respect to the ancient

---

18. Habermas, *Historical Jesus*, 187.
19. Habermas, *Historical Jesus*, 188.
20. Montgomery, *History, Law and Christianity*, 11–17.

manuscripts themselves. Such qualities as their number, age, and the consistency among them are taken into consideration.

Sir Frederic G. Kenyon, formerly the director and principal librarian of the British Museum, spoke to the bibliographical evidence:

> The interval ... between the dates of original composition and the earliest extant evidence [the earliest copies we have in our possession] becomes so small as to be in fact negligible, and the last foundation for any doubt that the Scriptures have come down to us substantially as they were written has now been removed. Both the authenticity and the general integrity of the books of the New Testament may be regarded as finally established.[21]

In addition, A. T. Robertson stated, "We have 13,000 [ancient] manuscript copies of portions of the New Testament. Besides all this, much of the New Testament can be reproduced from the quotations of the early Christian writers."[22] Among these earliest New Testament portions are "numerous papyri ... [dating back] to the end of the first century."[23] In addition, the New Testament has been reproduced by the Apostolic Fathers (earliest leaders in Christendom after the apostles) who wrote between AD 90–160. These sources provide "increasing evidence of their familiarity with and recognition of the authority of the New Testament writings."[24]

While comparing the record of the New Testament to other ancient works of antiquity, F. F. Bruce provides some examples. One of them is Caesar's *Gallic War*, which was composed between 58 and 50 BC, but among the approximate ten good manuscripts in our possession, the *oldest* is some nine hundred years later than the events recorded.[25] This demonstrates that the bibliographic evidence of the Bible is much more prevalent and more ancient than other works of that period. Another example is Tacitus's *Annals*, originally composed around AD 100. This work is represented by about a dozen extant copies (ten full copies and two partial), the oldest

---

21. Montgomery, *History, Law and Christianity*, 13.

22. Montgomery, *History, Law and Christianity*, 13. Robertson's work was published in 1925, and the number of ancient manuscripts discovered has only increased since that time.

23. Montgomery, *History, Law and Christianity*, 12.

24. Bruce, *New Testament Documents*, 13–14.

25. Bruce, *New Testament Documents*, 11.

copies dating back to the ninth century, over seven hundred years after the original composition.[26]

F. F. Bruce describes the result of the comparison between the New Testament documents and other works of antiquity: "The evidence for the New Testament writings is ever so much greater than the evidence for many writings of classical authors, the authenticity of which no-one dreams of questioning."[27]

From a theological perspective, these bibliographical details should be considered providentially. Stepping back, why would God permit such overwhelming bibliographical evidence? Perhaps he is interested in providing assurance to those who would receive his word that it is reliable and trustworthy.

Internal Evidence

Here, the historian allows the historical work to speak for itself, as it were, while taking note of the internal characteristics put forth in the documents. The ten characteristics mentioned above from Ron Rhodes are examples of internal evidence.

The most striking examples include eyewitness testimony, as this is one of the most important ways that evidence is weighed to this day in a court of law. What is fascinating about the quality of the New Testament eyewitnesses, however, is that many of them were hostile. Both friends and foes of the Lord Jesus Christ witnessed his person, his words, and his actions.

For example, what is recorded in the four gospels about Jesus Christ is the record of how both his followers and his enemies perceived him. The result is not what many would predict about Jesus Christ, since history is in the habit of not conforming to people's expectations. F. F. Bruce presents a summary of how Jesus Christ was perceived by first-century observers, perceptions backed up by a wide variety of eyewitnesses:

> Some traditional portrayals of him as a mild, inoffensive person are a travesty of the historical Jesus; if these portrayals corresponded to the reality, we could only wonder why anyone should have troubled to crucify him. The historical Jesus gave offence right and left. People found him a most disconcerting man. He

26. Bruce, *New Testament Documents*, 11.
27. Bruce, *New Testament Documents*, 10.

upset established notions of religious propriety. He spoke of God in terms of intimacy which sounded like blasphemy. He seemed to enjoy the most questionable company. He went out with open eyes upon a road which, in the view of all "sensible" folk, was bound to lead to disaster.[28]

Perhaps you've heard the saying "The truth hurts." When it does, it often highlights the quality of said truth. In the case of Jesus, the eyewitnesses for and against him witnessed his conflicts, accusations, trials, passion, and crucifixion. For the naysayer of the gospel, the truth hurts because the evidence is undeniable. For the sympathizer of Christ who also desires to sugarcoat the passion of Christ, the truth hurts because there is no denying what happened to Jesus when dealing with the sin of the world.

External Evidence

For external evidence, the historian considers historical materials outside the internal record and then seeks to establish whether these external materials either confirm or contradict what is recorded in the internal record. In support of the integrity of the word of God, there is a mound of external verifications of the accuracy of what is recorded. These are both written and nonwritten, such as what is substantiated by archeology.

The written external evidence substantiates much of the history recorded in the Holy Bible about Jesus Christ by the primary historians (the apostolic writers of the New Testament itself). Additionally, historians in the following traditions demonstrate consistency between the biblical record and history:

1. Jewish historians having composed the Mishnah law-code and the Talmud commentaries contribute to the reality of the historical person of Jesus Christ. In addition, before the Jewish literature was the testimony of Flavius Josephus, an acclaimed Jewish historian who also mentioned Christ and early Christians.[29]

2. Gentile historians including Greek and Roman writers also gave testimony to Christ and early Christians, including Tacitus, as mentioned

---

28. Bruce, *Defense of the Gospel*, 15.

29. See Bruce's chapter titled, "The Evidence of Early Jewish Writings" in Bruce, *New Testament Documents*, 102–15.

above. One of his accounts is not flattering, but it substantiates Christ and his followers in real history:

> Therefore, to scotch the rumour, Nero substituted as culprits, and punished with the utmost refinements of cruelty, a class of men, loathed for their vices, whom the crowd styled Christians, Christus, from whom they got their name, had been executed by sentence of the procurator Pontius Pilate when Tiberius was emperor. And the pernicious superstition was checked for a short time, only to break out afresh, not only in Judea, the home of the plague, but in Rome itself.[30]

It is this Christ—this "Christus"—who was the leader of Christians persecuted by Nero; this Christ who was executed under Pontius Pilate; and this Christ who was at the center of the "pernicious superstition," who is the Christ of real history. Thus, whenever Christians confess the creed, they confess Jesus Christ, who is not a fairy tale, myth, or figment of the imagination. Christians confess, "I believe . . . in Jesus Christ," the real Messiah in real human history, and his life was such that the Christian faith presents a way that is most compelling for the needs of humanity. And this, too, bears the mark of truth.

ICING ON THE HISTORICAL CAKE FOR JESUS

Prophecy is a word that must be defined and qualified. Called pastors proclaim prophecy in the sense of *forthtelling* the word of Christ given to the church. They herald God's word and announce the truth of that faith the church contends for, "once for all delivered to the saints" (Jude 3).

If, on the other hand, a pastor or any religious teacher comes along and claims to engage in prophecy that is not simply *forthtelling* but is *foretelling*, there is reason for concern. In the church today, the need for foretelling—or *predicting the future*—has passed. The need today is for faithful forthtelling of what God has revealed. The word of God itself keeps the distinction clear: "Long ago, at many times and in many ways, God spoke to our fathers by the prophets, but in these last days, he has spoken to us by his Son, whom he appointed the heir of all things through whom also he created the world" (Heb 1:1–2).

---

30. See Bruce's chapter titled, "The Evidence of Early Gentile Writers" in Bruce, *New Testament Documents*, 116–24. Bruce quotes Tacitus on page 121.

There was a time, however as the Scriptures teach, when God's mode of operation for delivering his revelation and teaching most certainly included foretelling. His called prophets in the Old Testament fulfilled their truth credentials (1) through the test of orthodoxy, demonstrating that what they proclaimed was consistent with God's word already in hand; and (2) through the test of truth, when what they foretold came to pass.

In other words, these prophets were engaged in demonstrating the power of God through the miracle of prophetic prediction that came to be fulfilled in the future.[31] And here we encounter one of the most powerful witnesses not only to the possibility of miracles but also assurance for the unique status of Jesus Christ as the Savior of the world.

The prophecies in the Old Testament concerning Jesus Christ before his birth and life on earth are, in fact, staggering to consider. Trying to establish a number for how many prophecies there are is debatable, but there are so many that one can align the summary predictions of these and get a clear view about the life and ministry of Jesus Christ many centuries before he was ever born. And this is true even if we conservatively stepped back from the hundreds of possible prophecies and settled for only sixty that are especially clear.[32]

The circumstances of fulfillment are of such a quality that they could not have been staged. For example, Christ had to come through an exact lineage, be born in a specific place, have magi come to worship him while still a toddler, and be born at a time when other children were slaughtered and when he might have been killed. He would also be introduced by John the Baptist, conduct miracles (quite a standard to live up to!), be rejected by his brethren, be betrayed by a friend, be sold for thirty pieces of silver, and be subjected to a form of capital punishment which did not exist during the time of prophecy.

It is stunning how out in the open this testimony of both the miraculous and the identity of the Lord Jesus Christ is. Some people ask, "If God is real, why doesn't he make himself more plainly seen?" What God has done for us through the historical record of prophetic fulfillment pertaining to Jesus Christ paints a picture for the world to see. Thus, God's reputation will

---

31. This is not to say that God's miraculous power is not still at work in the faithful forthtelling of his called servants. It is, and through it the Holy Spirit creates, sustains, and increases saving faith in Christ.

32. For this claim, I am indebted to Dr. Raymond Surburg's teaching during my time at Concordia Theological Seminary.

not be marred by the claim that he does not permit truth to be known, but rather people must take the blame for refusing to open their eyes and see.

CHAPTER 5 DISCUSSION GUIDE: CONTENDING FOR JESUS CHRIST OF REAL HISTORY

UNCOVER INFORMATION

1. What is the incarnation?
2. What are the two natures of Christ that must be maintained for our salvation?
3. What is a miracle?
4. Why did David Hume deny miracles?
5. What are the three evidences which demonstrate the reliability of Scripture?

DISCOVER MEANING

1. Why are the two natures of Christ necessary for our salvation?
2. Hume said that miracles are violations of the laws of nature. What is wrong with this definition?
3. How does the Holy Bible providing details about real times, places, events, and people speak to its reliability?
4. Why are unflattering stories about important Christian figures a favorable characteristic of Holy Scripture?
5. What is the significance of the creed including Pontius Pilate?

EXPLORE IMPLICATIONS

1. Finish these sentences: "If Christ is not fully God, then . . ."; "If Christ is not fully human, then . . ."
2. Why is it important that the church maintain the position of an open universe?

3. See the ten examples of Holy Scripture's historical and nonmythological character of God's word. Choose one you might especially like. How does it speak to Scriptures' overall quality?

4. What is the significance of God's word revealing such a long list of Saint Peter's failures and shortcomings?

5. Why is it advantageous for our Christian witness to embrace falsifiability?

6

Contending for Jesus, God Who Died

"I believe in God, . . . and in Jesus Christ, . . . [who] was **crucified**, **died**, and was **buried**."

GOD REALLY DIED

The fact that Jesus died cannot be downplayed. The creed cannot let go of the vital importance of ensuring that the believer in Jesus is confessing exactly that. To say that Jesus was crucified invariably implies that the One crucified died. After all, the Roman soldiers were expert executioners, and crucifixion itself was designed to achieve nothing less than death. However, to guarantee the outcome, the creed nevertheless cements the result: this One who was crucified, *died*. But even here, the creed will not leave an inkling of thinking otherwise: this One who was crucified and died, was also *buried, because that is what you do with dead people*. Burial is the punctuation mark: Jesus truly died. There can be no doubt.[1]

Why is this so vitally important to confirm? First, because there is no sense in taking comfort in his resurrection if he did not actually die. Second—and even more importantly—if he did not die, then the Lord of Life did not enter humanity's death. And if he did not enter our death, then

---

1. In fact, what is still to come in chapter 7—namely, the words "the third day"—is achieving an even *greater* assurance of his death. Anyone buried this long was dead beyond all doubt.

our death is still unconquered, and again, we are to be pitied more than all other people.²

But the Lord Jesus Christ *did* in fact enter death. To illustrate what happened when Christ entered our death, Luther uses a metaphor from an early church father, Gregory of Nyssa:

> The kingly authority of the divinity is given to Christ the man, not because of His humanity but because of His divinity. For the divinity alone created all things, without the cooperation of the humanity. Nor did the humanity conquer sin and death; but the hook that was concealed under the worm [referring to His dying human body], at which the devil struck, conquered and devoured the devil, who was attempting to devour the worm. Therefore the humanity would not have accomplished anything by itself; but the divinity, joined with the humanity, did it alone, and the humanity did it on account of the divinity.³

But to speak this way, because Holy Scripture does, enters a realm in speaking about God that no other religion on the planet dares speak. Christianity is the faith that believes, teaches, and confesses that God died. If the faithful pastor cannot proclaim that God died in Christ, then they have a problem.

Reason will not accommodate this thinking for one second. By nature, God cannot die, and yet in Christ who is God, God died. This is the paradoxical truth, and it cannot be watered down. The word of God proclaims to faithful leaders in the church, "Pay careful attention to yourselves and to all the flock, in which the Holy Spirit has made you overseers, to care for the church of God, which he obtained with his own blood" (Acts 20:28).

That is, this Jesus Christ who was crucified, died, and was buried is the God who humbles himself, makes himself low in ways that are otherwise unthinkable in the minds of people who insist that God can only be about power and beyond the shackles of human limitation. This God, Jesus, offends the sensibilities of what it means to be "God." He doesn't fit the human mold. And this is exactly why he should be considered trustworthy over and above all the grandiose and ostentatious ideas about God being

---

2. The resurrection of Christ did not in itself conquer death but was the inevitable manifestation of the fact that Christ conquered death on the cross of Calvary. The defeat of death occurred the split second Jesus died and entered death. When that happened the light of his divine life scattered the darkness of death. This is also why at the cross the first gospel of Gen 3:15 was fulfilled. On the cross, Jesus also defeated Satan.

3. Luther, *Galatians*, 267.

far, far removed from mere humans. The same God who was conceived, born, grew, and conducted his public ministry is the God who suffered and died.[4]

JESUS MADE HIMSELF NOTHING FOR A REASON

One of the most important Scriptures on the humiliation of Christ (the fact that he made himself low in human weakness) is Phil 2:5–8:

> Have this mind among yourselves, which is yours in Christ Jesus, who, though he was in the form of God, did not count equality with God a thing to be grasped, but emptied himself, by taking the form of a servant, being born in the likeness of men. And being found in human form, he humbled himself by becoming obedient to the point of death, even death on a cross.

The words, "emptied himself," do not imply that Jesus in any way compromised his divine nature. Rather, he permitted himself to genuinely experience the limitations of human nature, which he took upon his divinity. Christ *willed* to truly know the weaknesses of humanity, even to the point of *willing* himself to be able to taste death. The Solid Declaration of the *Book of Concord* states, "He kept it [the majesty of the divine nature] concealed in the state of His humiliation, and did not employ it always, but only when He wished."[5]

But why did he go to all this trouble? The reason is because he came to save all people, and to do that, Christ had to take our place under the law of God. And to do *that*, he had to be a true substitute in our place. He had to become like us in every way. He had to become our true brother. One of the ancient church fathers—namely, Gregory of Nazianzus—wrote, "For that which he has not assumed he has not healed; but that which is united to his Godhead is also saved."[6]

But if Christ also had possession of the divine nature at the same time, how could he *really* be like us? And this is precisely why Phil 2:5–8 is so vital. Jesus could *really* be like us because he "emptied himself." He humbled

---

4. Thus, Mary the mother of Christ was properly called by the early church (and the faithful church to this day) *Theotokos*, which means "God-bearer" or "Mother of God." The title is not to exalt Mary but to hold to the truth that the Jesus she bore was truly God in the flesh.

5. Solid Declaration, Article 8.26, McCain et al., *Lutheran Confessions*, 586.

6. Gregory of Nazianzus, *Letters* 101 (NPNF^2 7:440).

himself in respect to his divine power so thoroughly, that he was able to genuinely know our human weakness and limitations.

When I was a little boy, I idolized my brother Robert who was closest to my age, but still eight years older than me. I feel sorry for my brother when I think back because I must have driven him crazy. I always wanted to be around him and play with him. Of course, because he was a great big brother—and still is—he would oblige me, the little runt I was at the time.

One way he would do this was by wrestling with me, sometimes for long stretches of time. But allow me to put this "wrestling" in perspective. When I was eight, he was already sixteen playing football in high school. From one vantage point, there was no "wrestling" to be had. He was vastly stronger than I was. If he had wanted, he could have pinned me down in a second, and the wrestling would be over before it began.

However, my brother was generously accommodating to me, his little brother, making the wrestling interesting. The first thing he did was get on his knees. Now, we were almost eye to eye. The second thing he did was place his dominant hand behind his back. That is, he would wrestle me on his knees and with only his left hand.

After these significant adjustments, which he fully chose to make, we were off and running. I was a very aggressive kid, the kind that dove in and thought about it after the fact. I could circle around him and attack him from all angles as I enjoyed the use of *both* legs and *both* hands. To boot—as I mentioned—we went at it for a relatively long period of time.

The result? My brother, who was innately stronger than me, would experience a very thorough and tiring workout (as did I). He would be panting and sweating at the end of our matches. *And his panting and sweating were real, and not a sham. His was not imitation panting. His was no counterfeit sweat.* In fact, there were some moments when I probably hurt him. And if he expressed pain, it was no hoax. He had put himself in the position to experience the results of his true self-limitation.

This is what Jesus did, but in a far greater way. Christ did not merely get on his knees and put his right hand behind his back, but rather he took our flesh to experience our humanity. This is what the Holy Bible means by the fact that he "emptied himself."

There is a powerful scene in Holy Scripture that presents the betrayal and arrest of Jesus. When his arrestors put their hands on Christ, Saint Peter drew his sword and cut off the ear of the servant of the high priest. To this, Christ said to Saint Peter,

> Put your sword back into its place. For all who take the sword will perish by the sword. Do you think that I cannot appeal to my Father, and he will at once send me more than twelve legions of angels? (Matt 26:52–53)

On the cross of Calvary, Jesus most assuredly heard the mockery: "You who would destroy the temple and rebuild it in three days, save yourself! If you are the Son of God, come down from the cross" (Matt 27:40). He also heard, "He saved others; he cannot save himself. He is the King of Israel; let him come down from the cross, and we will believe in him" (Matt 27:42).

We would be wrong to think for a second that Jesus in fact was *unable* to come down from the cross. He was fully able, more than able as the One with all power and authority as God in the flesh, *but* he chose not to, he *willed* not to, he *humbled* himself, he *emptied* himself.

Why? Precisely so that as our Savior for us, he would be able to enter our death and do something about it, so that when we reach our temporal death, it will not spell our eternal death. This Jesus took our sin and our curse so that he could also take our death! Notice the substitutional descriptions of how people are saved from sin and death. In Christ, God the Father no longer sees the sin nor the curse upon those who trust in Jesus. This is because Jesus, in the eyes of God, took our sin and curse.

- "But he was pierced for our transgressions; he was crushed for our iniquities; upon him was the chastisement that brought us peace, and with his wounds we are healed" (Isa 53:5).
- "For our sake he made him to be sin who knew no sin, so that in him we might become the righteousness of God" (2 Cor 5:21).
- "Christ redeemed us from the curse of the law by becoming a curse for us—for it is written, 'Cursed is everyone who is hanged on a tree'" (Gal 3:13).

THE TRUE CHARACTER OF GOD
UNLIKE ANY OTHER "GOD"

The way people are rescued from sin and death in the Christian faith is diametrically opposed to any other religious system. It is a way that commences in compassion and mercy leading God to enter humility and weakness. By God entering these limitations, it demonstrates the crux of Christianity:

It is a faith or "religion" that does not demand the strength of people to be saved, but it insists upon the weakness of God to save people.

If natural religion means that people must achieve something for real and lasting life, the Christian faith turns that upside down. I try to avoid categorical statements, if possible, but sometimes they are appropriate. This is especially true in accordance with the law of noncontradiction, which states that if something is true, then the opposite of it is false.

What is at question is the way for life to endure. Jesus stated flatly, "I am the living bread that came down from heaven. If anyone eats of this bread, he will live forever. And the bread that I will give for the life of the world is my flesh" (John 6:51). Jesus also said, "I am the way, and the truth, and the life. No one comes to the Father except through me" (John 14:6).

Jesus did not speak this way out of ambition for self-aggrandizement or for political gain. He spoke this way out of love and to demonstrate that God's all-inclusive and universal way of salvation was achieved and offered through himself. This is not a matter of competition with other religions, nor is it for aggravating people who might suspect that exclusivism must always have an agenda—not at all. The gospel of Jesus Christ is both inclusive, in that it is good news for all people, and at the same time exclusive, in that this good news is something that Christ alone accomplished.

The possibility of what is inclusive and exclusive existing at the same time is not unreasonable. If someone needs water to survive, it means they rely upon a universal resource, something intended for all people to drink. At the same time, the water they drink is exclusively H_2O. It cannot be replaced with something else. People need a resource that is both inclusive, the universal answer for what they need to drink, that is at the same time an exclusive or completely unique resource for human survival. It would be silly to think that for the sake of political correctness, we could replace the water with motor oil or cyanide.[7]

So back to the law of noncontradiction. By making these assertions or claims, Jesus was clearly saying that with him we have real life, and without him we do not. If the immediate response to this is frustration or angst, then we might just as well feel this way for needing water instead of corn syrup.

But what makes Jesus' way of faith, religion, and real life different? It is, again, that the way of Jesus Christ is the way of the weakness of God

---

7. I present an elongated apologetic for the compatibility and complementarity of inclusivism and exclusivism in Espinosa, *Faith That Sees*, 137–48.

instead of the strength of people, which is illusory. The way of Christ is not for us to achieve or accomplish something. It is rather to see that in him, God does for people what they could never do for themselves. And that he does it by entering our weakness. He did it by *dying* for us.

In this way, we are given clarity for the analysis of world religions, sects (more recent), and cults or other movements (most recent): At the end of the day, do they advocate a form of natural religion for what people must do (prescriptions, requirements, disciplines, laws) or do they advocate what God has done for people (as a gift)? In the end, (1) natural religion relies upon what we do, and (2) the gospel relies upon what God does for us in Christ.

THE DEMANDS OF RELIGION ON PEOPLE

It is easy for people to think too much of themselves. One of my undergraduate professors said the middle letter in SIN is "I."[8] Indeed, it is easier to catch "I-itus" than it is to catch a common cold. It is like the person who is completely inconsiderate with a friend at dinner and says, "But that's enough of me talking about me, now *you* talk about me!"[9]

Pride was Lucifer's downfall, and pride was what Satan used to lure our first parents in paradise to rebel against God. Maybe you've heard the saying, "Pride goes before a fall." That word of wisdom comes from Prov 16:18.

So, it should not surprise us that things that appeal to our sense of accomplishment or earning a higher status are very attractive and appealing. These things stoke our pride and ego.

When I was growing up, my parents held up the importance of education (and I'm glad they did), but on my end of things, I sensed that if I achieved certain educational benchmarks, I would earn my parents' praise. Sometimes, we are driven to do things to address our insecurities and, sometimes, even our bare ambition.

In and of itself, ambition and even a kind of pride isn't all bad. After all, can a parent properly say they are proud of their child? Of course! Can a person be properly ambitious to hone their God-given skill? No doubt! However, on other occasions we are driven because our core sin assumes

---

8. Rev. Dr. Charles L. Manske, ca. 1984–1987.

9. My thanks goes out to my friend and brother in Christ, Doug Cavanaugh, for the corny joke.

that what we do is about us, and this kind of presumption can easily be applied to faith and religion.[10]

The problem of the various forms of natural religion is that they feed into this mistaken presumption: real life is something that people who die can accomplish. We can't. And Jesus avoids this false message like the plague.

Most religions, however, buy into the mistaken presumption in one form or another. It is important to understand that we are not conveying that there is no truth in other religions. That would be going too far. Again, because all people have natural revelation and the natural knowledge of God is universal, it is easy to find aspects of truth in just about any religious system. At issue, however, is the question, How is real life had? Will I be directed to myself, or will I be directed to what the God who is really there has done for me?

Hinduism presents "Salvation through 'endless' cycles of birth-death-rebirth (*samsara*), controlled by one's actions (*karma*), and ending in deliverance (*moksha*) from *samsara* and the material."[11] So, how does one address karma so as to achieve ultimate deliverance? Enter the Four Ways/Paths: (1) *karma-marga* (work/action), (2) *jnana-marga* (knowledge), (3) *bhakti-marga* (devotion/meditation), and (4) *raja-marga* (or *yoga*—insight, physical discipline). If *dharma* (duty, acted out according to karma) is properly carried out, then rebirth to a higher caste can be attained. Ultimately, *nirvana* can be achieved.[12]

Hinduism, which is a major world religion with over one billion adherents, is a clear natural religion. To achieve deliverance and to reach nirvana is completely on the adherent. When will the disciple of Hinduism achieve enough, and the right, karma? When will the follower master the four ways/paths? It is understandable if achieving some level of assurance seems unattainable.

And while there are many gods in Hinduism, Brahma is "the Creator," "Lord of All," an abstract deity.[13] He leaves one with a way of life, and beyond that, it is up to the person to do the very best they can possibly do.

---

10. Luther referred to this problem as "the presumption of righteousness," when we presume that we can make ourselves righteous, which is fatal assumption that leads us to depend on our efforts over and above trusting in God. See Luther's exposition of Gal 3:19 in Luther, *Galatians*, 304–23.

11. Manske and Harmelink, *World Religions Today*, 2.

12. Manske and Harmelink, *World Religions Today*, 2.

13. Manske and Harmelink, *World Religions Today*, 2.

PART II | SECOND ARTICLE OF THE CREED

Buddhism is another major world religion with over a half-billion adherents on planet earth. In the case of Buddhism, salvation is "the goal to overcome karma (the effects of works), escape samsara (rebirth-cycle), and obtain nirvana (final-enlightened-happy-state)."[14] How is this achieved? Again, a classical approach to natural religion is blatantly obvious: one is to find the middle way/path between hedonism and asceticism which includes grasping the four noble truths: (1) all life is suffering (*dukkha*); (2) all suffering is from craving (*tanha*); (3) release is possible through non-craving, therefore no suffering; and (4) follow the Eightfold Path, no craving–no suffering.

The Eightfold Path is straightforward: (1) right views, (2) right aspirations, (3) right speech, (4) right conduct, (5) right livelihood, (6) right effort, (7) right mindfulness, and (8) right meditation.[15]

And with this we have another powerful example of natural religion relying on the person who follows Buddhism. What is more, there is no identified ultimate "god" in Buddhism, cutting off the hope for helpful intervention.

Even larger than both Hinduism and Buddhism is Islam, whose adherents are identified with the words "Muslim" or "Moslem," with its greatest earthly leader and prophet being Muhammad (AD 570–632). Even the word itself, "Islam," indicates the natural religion emphasis of this faith system. It means "submission to the will of Allah." Twenty percent of earth's population is Muslim.[16]

Allah is the one and only god of Islam who will judge all souls at the end of time.[17] Among the messengers of Allah are twenty-eight prophets, including Jesus Christ, whose divinity is denied. The most important teaching of Islam is "the perfect peace when one's life is surrendered to God." This can be achieved through the Five Pillars of Islam: (1) repetition of the creed (*Shahadah*), "There is no God but Allah; Muhammad is the messenger of Allah"; (2) prayer—five times each day (*Salat*)—while facing Mecca (the holiest city of Islam); (3) alms to the poor, or poor tax (*Zakat*), as opposed to voluntary almsgiving (*Sadaqa*); (4) fasting in the month of Ramadan (*Siyam*) while eating at night only; and (5) a pilgrimage (*Al-Hajj*)

---

14. Manske and Harmelink, *World Religions Today*, 18.
15. Manske and Harmelink, *World Religions Today*, 18.
16. Rhodes, *10 Things*, 8–9.
17. Manske and Harmelink, *World Religions Today*, 81.

to Mecca once in a lifetime.[18] It should not be forgotten that *Jihâd*, the duty to fight all unbelievers, also marks faithfulness to Islam (though this can be variously interpreted).

Nevertheless, what is clear once again is the standard of natural religion: mustering the strength for the follower to do what they must to achieve heaven and to avoid condemnation.

All of these are examples of self-salvation, and therefore occasions for the most popular concept of religion of what one must accomplish, achieve, merit, or deserve. All of these are examples of what is precisely opposite of what Jesus Christ has brought to humanity.

BUT DOESN'T JESUS TEACH ABOUT HOW TO LIVE?

It would be easy at this juncture to experience a little confusion. Doesn't the Christian faith advocate the keeping of the Ten Commandments, and didn't Jesus himself teach what he referred to as the greatest commandments? Indeed, he did.

- The Greatest Commandment: "You shall love the Lord your God with all your heart and with all your soul and with all your mind" (Matt 22:37).
- The Second Greatest Commandment: "You shall love your neighbor as yourself" (Matt 22:39).

Jesus didn't hesitate to communicate the enormous import of these: "On these two commandments depend all the Law and the Prophets" (Matt 22:40). Doesn't this lead straight back to natural religion? Not so fast.

God also makes it extraordinarily clear as to the purpose of the Law (and Commandments) in the Holy Bible. Saint Paul provides this lucid insight: "For by works of the law no human being will be justified in his sight, since through the law comes knowledge of sin" (Rom 3:20).

Thus, the primary purpose of God's holy law clearly taught in the Ten Commandments and the two greatest commandments was and is to show people that they fall short of the standards of the One, True, and Holy God. Jesus elaborated on this state of affairs in his great Sermon on the Mount:

> You have heard that it was said to those of old, "You shall not murder; and whoever murders will be liable to judgment." But I say to

18. Manske and Harmelink, *World Religions Today*, 81.

> you that everyone who is angry with his brother will be liable to judgment; whoever insults his brother will be liable to the council; and whoever says, "You fool! will be liable to the hell of fire. . . . You have heard that it was said, "You shall not commit adultery." But I say to you that everyone who looks at a woman with lustful intent has already committed adultery with her in his heart." (Matt 6:21–22, 27–28)

Who does not get angry at other people and does not have sinful desire? These are rhetorical questions of course. The answers are "no one has not," and "everyone has." Jesus therefore was and is teaching that all people sin and violate the commandments of God. He also taught about a core problem all people have (recall our discussion above in chapter 1), that core problem he once vividly described as he related the condition of the human heart to the actions which proceed from it:

> Hear and understand: it is not what goes into the mouth that defiles a person, but what comes out of the mouth; this defiles a person. . . . But what comes out of the mouth proceeds from the heart, and this defiles a person. For out of the heart comes evil thoughts, murder, adultery, sexual immorality, theft, false witness, slander. These are what defile a person. (Matt 15:10, 18–19)

That is, the Law and Commandments of God serve as a diagnostic. They are a way for us to be able to recognize what sin is and what sin does. It turns from God while turning inward toward oneself, and then it commits acts contrary to the will of God. In short, God gives his commandments not so that we would try to save ourselves, but so that we would realize that we can't.

In Holy Scripture which puts forth the teaching of the Christian faith, God gives his Law and Commandments not for us enter natural religion but instead so that we would recognize its bankruptcy.

That is, God is acting as a good doctor. We go in to see our doctor, and he conducts an exam. Then, he pronounces a diagnosis. The news might not be good, but even if it is bad, we are put into a position to have something done about it. If, however, we are never aware we have a problem, why on earth would we be interested in a cure?

This is precisely what God is doing with his Law and Commandments. Through these, we know that we need God and that natural religion—resting on our own steam—will never get the job done.

There is, of course, more to the story: when God provides the answer to our breaking his Law and Commandments, his "cure" is his Son, Jesus Christ. This includes all that Christ did to take our sin from us, putting it on himself, removing our curse from us to be counted as his curse, and permitting his stripes for our sin so that we could be healed.

In doing this, Christ puts us into a new status. We are the beloved children of God for whom the Son of God spilled his blood to pay for our sins (the cost of our having rebelled against God and breaking his Law and Commandments). This makes our value in the eyes of God as we trust in Jesus inestimable. This value moves God to adopt us as his children through his word and sacraments, and when he does, he gifts the followers of Jesus Christ with the Holy Spirit (also known as the Spirit of Christ and the Spirit of God).

When the child of God who now trusts and depends on Jesus Christ has the Spirit of Christ, then they are moved to live the life God calls his children to live. Yes, there is a real *doing* here, but with important distinctions.

1. It is not a doing for merit.
2. It is not a doing for self-salvation.
3. It does not belong to the arena of natural religion.
4. It is a doing that does not consider God's commandments as burdensome (1 John 5:3).
5. It is a doing generated by the Holy Spirit and prepared by God for us to do (Gal 5:22–23, Eph 2:10).
6. It is a doing that demonstrates a new creation, not because it must in terms of obligation, but because it must in terms of what it *is* (consider the sun: it does not shine and radiate heat out of obligation, but it must because of what it *is*).
7. It is the doing of Jesus Christ in and through his people.

That is, in Christ natural religion is vanquished. No longer does a person *do* to *get*, but they do because they have already received.

JESUS MOVES US TO DESIRE HIS REAL LIFE

When I was going through college and seminary, I had several jobs, but among them was working in retail, selling electronic equipment and computers. It was important for me to know my products and to be ready to answer questions and be prepared to elaborate on the benefits. But there were some items that were so desirable that I did very little selling because, frankly, they sold themselves. There are some things in life like that. In fact, there are some things so glorious that there is no selling at all. In fact, the only thing keeping a needy person from holding to the Lord Jesus Christ is for that person to deny their neediness.

But why would anyone want to do that? If we step back to look at the big picture, why should it be surprising that the God who freely created the universe and every other aspect of life would not continue to desire to give—and give freely—even eternal, lasting, and real life that continues by knowing him as our loving and merciful God? Why would he suddenly switch gears? Why start life by creating us and then make it practically impossible for us to continue in life illuminated by his love?

Why confess the God who is there, who created us, and founded life, to then turn around and insist on a "god" who gives us a laundry list of what must be done to avoid reprobation?

Instead, the true God known in Jesus Christ goes to great lengths to show his compassion and love. He is not the God who sits atop a mountain waiting for us to drag ourselves up to him. He is rather the true God who comes down the mountain to us even to the extent of becoming our brother. The writer to the Hebrews provides this amazing revelation of who Jesus is:

> Since therefore the children share in flesh and blood, he himself likewise partook of the same things, that through death he might destroy the one who has the power of death, that is, the devil, and deliver all those who through fear of death were subject to lifelong slavery. For surely it is not angels that he helps, but he helps the offspring of Abraham. Therefore he had to be made like his brothers in every respect, so that he might become a merciful and faithful high priest in the service of God, to make propitiation[19] for the sins of the people. For because he himself has suffered, when tempted, he is able to help to help those who are being tempted. (Heb 2:14–18)

John W. Kleinig is superb in elaborating on this teaching of Christ for us from the book of Hebrews:

---

19. *Propitiation* is what Christ did on the cross as he absorbed or deflected the wrath of God we deserved for our sins, so God's wrath never reached us but fell only upon him, our saving substitute.

The capacity for sympathy that he gained from sharing fully in human weakness and suffering gives him the ability to graciously "help" people in their suffering. He grants sensitive help instead of burdening them with greater demands. He understands their weaknesses, since he himself has experienced the full extent of human weakness (4:15). Thus the kinship of Jesus with his brothers includes his ongoing involvement with them in temptation. His own experience of temptation and suffering equips him to intercede on their behalf with sympathy and compassion (4:15–16; 7:25). By virtue of his suffering, God's Son has become a truly merciful High Priest.[20]

Indeed, the God who is there has the capacity for sympathy towards us precisely because he shared fully in human weakness and suffering. That word *sympathy* is not just describing a feeling but an active doing which comes alongside the person who is burdened. He does not prescribe to us as we live in his life what he has not already done and continues to do for us: "Bear one another's burdens, and so fulfill the law of Christ" (Gal 6:2). But again, who is the One who bore our burden and continues to help us with our burden? It is the True God, Jesus Christ.

The author of the New Testament book of Hebrews continues to describe Christ in this fashion:

> Since then we have a great high priest who has passed through the heavens, Jesus, the Son of God, let us hold fast our confession. For we do not have a high priest who is unable to sympathize with our weaknesses, but one who in every respect has been tempted as we are, yet without sin. Let us then with confidence draw near to the throne of grace, that we may receive mercy and find grace to help in time of need. (Heb 4:14–16)

Again, Kleinig is exquisite:

> Their Priest can do what no other priest could do; he uses his power to sympathize with them in a truly helpful way. He does not just feel what they feel and as they feel. Rather, as the Greek verb συμπαθῆσαι, "to sympathize" (4:15), implies, he suffers with them. He joins them in their suffering and suffers what they suffer. Their suffering is from the weaknesses that come from sin against God, the physical and spiritual infirmities that disable them and disqualify them from God's presence. . . . Jesus is able to "sympathize with" us in a way that is neither condescending nor

---

20. Kleinig, *Hebrews*, 143.

unhelpful, because he too has suffered and "been tempted in every way like us." ... Since he is without sin, he can suffer with sinners in order to take on their sin. ... No one else can do that! No one else can exercise that kind of sympathy in suffering! He bridges the gulf between heaven and earth, because he joins sinful humanity, perilously and at great cost, in their alienation from God, in order to rejoin them safely with God. He goes so low so that he can raise them so high.[21]

JESUS HAS ALWAYS BEEN THE SAME

The Christian faith has as its foundation the Old Testament. It is a popular mistake when even Christians will refer to the Pentecost event recorded in Acts 2 as "the birthday of the Christian church." The True and Only Wise God has always been, and the Holy Scriptures which begin to reveal him as Father, Son, and Holy Spirit begin at Gen 1:1. The moment God spoke in Gen 1:3, "Let there be light," the Word of God—the Speaking of God—was in action, and who is that Word? It is Christ, the Word who became flesh (John 1:1, 14).

Thus, Christians have always held to the Old Testament as the word of God and would never consider the Holy Bible complete without the Old Testament.

Therefore, if the True God is eternal, and he makes himself known through humility and compassion, shouldn't we expect his tenderness and mercy to also be conveyed in the Old Testament? Undoubtedly. And it is. Here is a short sampling of Scripture from the Old Testament:

- "As far as the east is from the west, so far does he remove our transgressions from us" (Ps 103:12).
- "I, I am he who blots out your transgressions for my own sake, and I will not remember your sins" (Isa 43:25).
- "For I will forgive their iniquity, and I will remember their sin no more" (Jer 31:34b).
- "The steadfast love of the Lord never ceases; his mercies never come to an end; they are new every morning; great is your faithfulness" (Lam 3:22–23).

---

21. Kleinig, *Hebrews*, 231–32.

- "Who is a God like You, pardoning iniquity and passing over transgression for the remnant of His inheritance? He does not retain His anger forever, because He delights in steadfast love. He will again have compassion on us; He will tread our iniquities under foot. You will cast all our sins into the depths of the sea" (Mic 7:18–19).

Then of course is one of the most famous psalms of all time, Ps 23. It gives sublime comfort as it begins, "The Lord is my shepherd; I shall not want" (Ps 23:1). This one verse teaches us that because the Lord lovingly and tenderly looks over us, we shall not lack anything we need in our lives. And the image of the Shepherd is itself an image of God who dwells with his people, not above them. He is among us through the valley of life and the valley of death. He is right there, with his rod (to protect) and his staff (to guide).

But what of the unique work of the Lord Jesus Christ on the cross to be the God who came in weakness to save us even and especially through death? Is this teaching reserved only for the New Testament? Much to the contrary, it is perhaps most thoroughly presented in Isa 53. Just how far did the Shepherd of all people go? The Scriptures teach, "All we like sheep have gone astray; we have turned—everyone—to his own way; and the Lord has laid on him the iniquity of us all" (Isa 53:6). It was this One who "poured out his soul with death and was numbered with the transgressors [recall the two thieves, one on his left and the other on his right]; yet he bore the sin of many and makes intercession for the transgressors" (Isa 53:12b).

This is the True and Only Wise God who comes to us. He ventures to earth and does not wait for us to climb to heaven. His humble presence is presented in a most sublime way in Gen 32. Jacob is filled with fear at the prospect of meeting his brother Esau (having previously stolen his birthright), so he "wrestles" with God. Then God tells Jacob to let him go (Gen 32:6), to which Jacob replies to Almighty God, "I will not let you go unless you bless me" (Gen 32:6).

What bare audacity! What incredible confidence in the mercy of God! What comfort in knowing the God who comes to his children in their great weakness! Luther commented,

> In this manner God is conquered when faith does not leave off, is not wearied, and does not cease but presses and urges on.... This is the power and strength of the Spirit. Christ, while still wrestling with Jacob and with His omnipotence concealed, wants to be dismissed, but Jacob replies: "I will not let you go, unless you

bless me.... I will not let you go unless you retract your judgment concerning me and give me the testimony that I have been blessed before God."[22]

How can children of God have this quality of confidence? Because they know that in Christ, God has come to join them in their weakness and even in their death. Therefore, God will help them through all things so that their weakness is turned to strength, and their death turned to life.

BUT WHAT ABOUT . . .

If the God who is there delights to enter our weakness, is unashamed to become our brother, is unafraid to enter our death, and is so loving and merciful, then what about the times in the Old Testament that we encounter the Hebrew word and concept *charam*, which means to devote to God and to destroy completely? In these instances, God commanded the armies of Israel to wipe away enemy cities with *everything* that was in them (e.g., Num 21, Deut 2, Deut 3, Josh 6, and Josh 11). Why did God do this?

First, regarding both the instances of *charam* as well as instances of miracles, sometimes people get the impression that both were regular and frequent occurrences in the life of the people of God. Nothing could be further from the truth.

In every case, these were exceptions and not the rule of the actions of God. God permitted miracles at times to emphasize the seismic lesson for Israel and the world. For example, the miracles surrounding the ministry of Moses were for the specific purpose of showing the superiority (and therefore, trustworthiness) of the True God over and above the false pantheon of the Egyptians.

Second, both the miracles and *charam* demonstrated the significance of Israel being the chosen nation of God in the Old Testament. Why was this so important? Because through this nation, God was sending through their lineage and seed, the Messiah-Christ, the Savior of the world.

The same thing is true regarding *charam*. It is not to be supposed that God had no mercy on non-Israelites. In fact, God had so much mercy on non-Israelites that some are even included in the genealogy of the Christ. For example, among his great-grandmothers was Ruth, not an Israelite but a Moabitess, and Rahab, a prostitute of Jericho, one of the cities of the

---

22. Luther, *Deuteronomy*, 139.

Canaanites (Matt 1). Rather, *charam* was commanded by God for the astronomically important event of the establishment of and the protection of the Israelites in the promised land. If the Messiah would come through them for the salvation of all people, nothing could be allowed to compromise their existence.

In the case of *charam*, God fully employed his omniscience to know what people could never know. We cannot peer into the hearts of people, but God can. So, what did he see in the Canaanites who fell victim to *charam*? God knows that in some instances people can become so hardened and so rebellious that they will never turn. Again, this is something we cannot know about a person. Christians are never to give up hope on anyone. But again, God knows what we do not.

He knew that these people dedicated to darkness and the demonic were able to destroy Israel, if not militarily, then through spiritual influence and infiltration. That is, *charam* is not a cheap version of "just war" or an excuse for rampant *Jihâd*. It was instead a means for preventing the destruction of his own people through the onslaught of evil—which God could clearly see—in the Canaanites.

Sometimes evil can be that rampant. Recall that evil is no mere synonym for sin but is the deliberate breaking out of sin against God and against people. People driven by evil take delight in destruction. Evil brings delight to hearts determined to harm others. Such was the spiritual condition of the Canaanites. God knew what they would have done to his people, thus not only compromising his holy nation but most importantly, threatening the life of the Messiah, the Savior of the world.

I am a pastor, and I am also a black belt in traditional taekwondo. When I assist in teaching children at our martial arts school, we tell them if they are ever attacked, they should *run*. We should never have any desire to fight. Having said that, if I saw a man attacking one of my little grandchildren, one of my children, or my wife, I would not hesitate—out of love—to defend my family. This is what love would do when loved ones are threatened.

We can have funny ideas about love sometimes, but true love will protect the beloved. Sometimes, that will not be what we want to see, but that does not mean that the love in play is not genuine. The God who is there, the real God, cares so much for his people that he will not only sympathize with them, join them in their weakness, but he will also protect them. And believers should never be ashamed of that but should hold this truth as endearing and priceless.

All this describes Jesus. When he saw his people weeping over the death of Lazarus, the Holy Scriptures record, "He was deeply moved in his spirit and greatly troubled" (John 11:33), and it would not be going too far to say that in the most holy way possible, he was angry. He knew what the enemies of his people, sin, death, and the devil had done to Lazarus, also causing the grieving of his loved ones. Jesus was determined to do something about it. He wanted to go to the tomb of Lazarus to deal with the enemies who had caused so much pain to his people. That is, Jesus went to war for us. Even to the extent that he himself was devoted to God. He conducted *charam* upon himself so that he would be the One to have *his* life destroyed. And when he did, he entered the fray and came out victorious over death. He became alive after having died. To this teaching of the Apostles' Creed we now proceed.

CHAPTER 6 DISCUSSION GUIDE: CONTENDING FOR JESUS, GOD WHO DIED

UNCOVER INFORMATION

1. How was Jesus, who is God, able to die?
2. Gregory of Nazianzus taught, "That which [Jesus] has not assumed He has not _____." Therefore, Jesus had to be like us in _____ way (except without sin).
3. Why did Jesus humble/empty himself?
4. What basic sin was the devil's downfall?
5. How does the Old Testament describe God's love and mercy?

DISCOVER MEANING

1. What did Luther mean by "the hook that was concealed under the worm"?
2. Regarding the analogy of the author as a boy having wrestled his big brother, how does this illustrate the true humiliation of Christ for us?
3. What is "natural religion"?
4. What does it mean that Jesus sympathized with our weaknesses?
5. What was *charam*, and why did God command it?

EXPLORE IMPLICATIONS

1. Why is natural religion bankrupt and that which can give no certainty of salvation?
2. How does Jesus emptying himself speak of his love for the Father and for us?
3. If following God's law is not how we are saved, then why are Christians nevertheless committed to keeping God's law anyway?
4. How does the record of Jacob wrestling with God teach us about what saving faith *does*?
5. Despite the seeming contradiction, how does *charam* actually demonstrate God's love for his people?

7

Contending for Jesus, the Death of Death

"I believe in God, . . . and in Jesus Christ. . . . The third day
he rose again from the dead."

CHRIST WHO ENLIVENS DUST, MUD, AND CLAY

When considering the resurrection of Jesus Christ, it may be easy to get stuck on the possibility and likelihood of a mere man dying and then rising. In other words, we could conduct this thought line: *Jesus was a man as we know men, with all the physiological considerations in connection to a man, any man, and we know that when cells die, they remain dead.*

But this is where we limit our considerations. The Christian faith does not hesitate for a second to confess that Jesus Christ was 100 percent a man, completely our brother, with a human nature as much as anyone reading this. Furthermore, his human nature was completely necessary for winning our salvation. Recall our citation of Gregory of Nazianzus above and in shorthand here: "Whatever Jesus did not take on, he did not redeem." His was a human body, a human mind, and a human soul. He was able to be our true substitute in life and death.

This man was, at the same time, unlike any other person. That is, there is a supreme additive to the equation for considering the resurrection of Jesus Christ. The question now becomes, "Is God able to take the cells which have died, and rejuvenate them?" It is not unlike asking another question which we considered above about God as Creator: "Is God able to create out of nothing?" The author to the Hebrews asserts, "By faith we understand that the universe was created by the word of God, so that what is seen was not made out of things that are visible" (Heb 11:3).

But let's take our consideration from starting with nothing to starting with something; let us graduate from nothing to soil, mud, or clay: "Then the Lord God formed the man of dust from the ground and breathed into his nostrils the breath of life, and the man became a living creature" (Gen 2:7).

If God is the God who is there, why would this be difficult for him? In the Holy Scriptures, he is making connections for us so that we might consider that what he can do with dust, he can do with dead cells.

You might recall the earlier observation above that miracles—like *charam*—were not common place. There were seasons in the world's history in which certain events and persons received punctuated attention for a reason. God was telling the world, "This is a critical juncture in human history for the salvation of the world, so I will mark it with signs, and the signs will be for people to take notice."

One of those junctures was the three-year public ministry of the Lord Jesus while he walked the earth with his disciples. The miracles deliberately came in three categories so that people might know who this man was. These included miracles showing

1. God's power over disease and death,
2. God's power over the demonic,
3. God's power over nature.

There was nothing haphazard about the miracles of the Lord Jesus Christ. Much to the contrary, during the interrogations of Christ leading up to his crucifixion, Pilate sent Jesus to Herod, and Herod wanted to be entertained. "When Herod saw Jesus, he was very glad, for he had long desired to see him, and he was hoping to see some sign done by him" (Luke 23:8).

If Jesus had desired, he could have put on a show the likes of which Herod had never seen. But the Lord was not a circus performer, and he was not going to do anything to divert his goal and desire of being faithful to his mission. Nothing would keep him from the cross to atone for the sins of the world.

When he was not before the powerful figures of the world, however, he conducted his signs appropriately, strategically, and for the time and place for which they were meant to be seen. They were designed to correspond to his preaching. For example, Jesus had clearly proclaimed,

> And as Jesus reclined at table in the house, behold, many tax collectors and sinners came and were reclining with Jesus and his disciples. And when the Pharisees saw this, they said to his disciples, "Why does your teacher eat with tax collectors and sinners?" But when he heard it, he said, "Those who are well have no need of a physician, but those who are sick. Go and learn what this means: 'I desire mercy, and not sacrifice.' For I came not to call the righteous, but sinners." (Matt 9:10–13)

Thus, Jesus' miraculous signs were for consistency with his message. He did not do his signs for the world of power and prestige, but for the world suffering from the impact of sin and its symptoms of disease, agony, suffering, and death. His signs were not for the powerful (for those who thought of themselves that way) but for the weak (for those who were realistic about the human condition).

So, for these Jesus gave signs. There were two occasions that stand out not only for the signs themselves, but for the phenomenal examples of faith held in the hearts of those who sought Jesus. One of those two was the Syrophoenician woman (Mark 7:24–30), also referred to as the Canaanite woman (Matt 15:21–28). Her faith in Christ was so powerful that Jesus announced, "O woman, great is your faith! Be it done for you as you desire" (Matt 15:28). At that moment, Jesus healed her daughter who was not present in that scene. The distance didn't matter.

The other occasion of the great faith of the one who received a sign from Jesus was the Roman centurion (Matt 8:5–13, Luke 7:1–10). Matthew describes the centurion coming to Jesus, but in fact his coming was through his emissaries, as Luke is more specific. The centurion was humbly asking the Savior to heal his servant. He knew on account of Christ's power, he could do so without even coming into the centurion's quarters where his servant was lying. Jesus was astounded by his faith and did not hesitate to conduct a sign. Luke records, "When Jesus heard these things [the centurion's request without need for Jesus to come], he marveled at him, and turning to the crowd that followed him, said, 'I tell you, not even in Israel have I found such faith.' And when those who had been sent returned to the house, they found the servant well" (7:9–10).

But there were other signs that got Jesus into the trenches. He interacted with bodies, even some overcome by dead cells. One of those interactions takes us back to Genesis. God had first used dust, clay, or mud to make a man. On a later day God in the flesh took some mud again to heal.

> As he passed by, he saw a man blind from birth. And His disciples asked him, "Rabbi, who sinned, this man or his parents, that he was born blind?" Jesus answered, "It was not that this man sinned, or his parents, but that the works of God might be displayed in him. We must work the works of him who sent me while it is day; night is coming, when no one can work. As long as I am in the world, I am the light of the world. Having said these things, he spit on the ground and made mud with the saliva. Then he anointed the man's eyes with the mud and said to him, "Go, wash in the pools of Siloam" (which means Sent). So he went and washed and came back seeing. (John 9:1–7)

Jesus had used mud before. When the power of God touches mud or clay, he fashions something that can live. John the Baptist said as much when he called people to turn from their sins and to believe in the coming Savior: "I tell you, God is able from these stones to raise up children for Abraham" (Matt 3:9). Dust, mud, and stones—or nothing at all—is all God needs to bring life.

During Jesus' public ministry, there were those whose dusty bodies had died that Jesus encountered. Jesus raised from death (1) the widow of Nain's son (Luke 7:11–17), (2) Jairus's daughter (Luke 8:40–56), and (3) Lazarus of Bethany (John 11). There were a handful of nature signs. There were also a handful of signs over the demonic, and a handful over diseases. Just enough. These were signs that shouted, "Listen to this One!" "Listen to him!" "Hear him!" "Trust him!" "Follow him!"

The widow was lowly in the culture, but Jesus intervened while she grieved having lost her only son. She was not a king like Herod, nor was she asking for a sign. Jesus simply had compassion on her and knew that this was the right time.

Jairus was a man of faith, a leader of a local synagogue, and he did not consider himself great as he went "falling at Jesus' feet" (Luke 8:41), begging him to heal his daughter about twelve years old. She died as Jesus was still on his way, but the God who is there knew that this was the right time for a sign. This happened even as people around the dead girl laughed when he finally arrived and said that she was only "sleeping" (because that is how innocuous death is to those who belong to God).

And then there was Jesus' friend Lazarus, the brother of two other friends who had welcomed Jesus into their home, Mary and Martha. Jesus witnessed the deep grieving of the sisters over their brother and the others also grieving. Jesus was moved with so much compassion that he also wept (John 11:35). This time, however, much more time had passed. Lazarus had been in his tomb for four days, but Jesus said to Martha, "Did I not tell you that if you believed you would see the glory of God?" (John 11:40). Then the sign came. God had come and once again he acted upon the dead dust.

This One, with God's power because he was and is God enfleshed, was also the One who entered his own death. Interestingly, when Jesus was being mocked while he died on the cross, at least one of the mockers shouted, "Save yourself!" (Matt 27:40). As mentioned above, he could have, but he would not.

Nothing would curtail his atonement for the sins of the world. He loved the Father too much for that, and he loved all of us too much for that. However, this is not to say that—eventually—he did not save himself. After all, the same incarnate God, God with us as Isaiah called him (Isa 7:14), who touched the dust and clay of others, could do the same for his own dust and clay.

According to Holy Scripture, the Holy Spirit raised Jesus from the dead (Rom 8:11). Furthermore, the word teaches that the Father raised his Son, Jesus, from the dead (Heb 13:20, Eph 1:20). But should it surprise us that the resurrection of Christ is also attributed to Christ raising himself? "Jesus answered them, 'Destroy this temple, and in three days I will raise it up. . . . He was speaking about the temple of his body" (John 2:19, 21). There has never been a time that the Lord of life has not had power over death so that dead cells are as the dust he breathed into to create life to begin with.

CHRIST THE DEVIL'S DEVIL

Given this power over death, Luther understood the implications against all that threatens us with despair and death. Luther could write this way because he knew the Christ who defeated death. Speaking to the tyrant of the law of God which accuses us of sin, brings death, and delights the devil who works against us Luther wrote,

> Law, if you are able to bite me, bind me, and plague me, I will put another Law above you, that is, another tyrant and tormentor, who

will accuse you, bind you, and oppress you in turn. You are indeed my tormentor. But I have another tormentor, namely, Christ. He will torment you all the way. When you have been tormented all the way by Him, then I am free. Likewise, if the devil whips me, I have a stronger devil, who will whip him in turn. And when the more powerful devil battles and conquers the powerful one, I am set free. Thus grace is a Law—not to me, because it does not bind me, but to my Law; this it binds in such a way that it cannot bind me any longer. . . . See this very joyous duel: sin battling sin, in order to become righteousness to me; death battling against death, in order that I might have life. For Christ is my devil against the devil, that I might be a son of God; He destroys hell, that I might have the kingdom of heaven.[1]

Christ, the devil's devil, is also the death of death. And if this is the case—if God has been this gracious and good to all humanity—then it comes as no shock that he has left immaculate imprints of this life-changing event.

THE REASON WE CARE

Buddhism suggests eliminating desire that suffering might also be eliminated. Certainly, there are many things that we ought not desire because so many things in this world are designed for misery. For example, alcohol is commended in God's word for celebrations, the Holy Sacrament of the Altar / Holy Communion, for medicinal purposes, and even to help people filled with overflowing despair: "Give strong drink the one who is perishing, and wine to those in bitter distress; let them drink and forget their poverty and remember their misery no more" (Prov 31:6–7). But to desire strong drink for the purpose of debauchery takes a good thing and turns it into something very bad indeed.

There is, however, one thing God has designed us to *strongly* desire: *life*. In fact, it is something we crave. Even the person who despairs of life is not denying their desire for life, but their desire to escape what is causing pain in their life. And it was for life that God does what he does.

He created to give life; he gives good gifts to preserve life. When life went astray on account of our denying our God of life, he did not stop blessing us with life but came to restore life. Life is at the crux of all that Christ

---

1. Luther, *Galatians*, 164.

does for us. Thus he said, "The thief comes only to steal and kill and destroy [the works of Satan]. I came that they may have life and have it abundantly" (John 10:10).

Thus, God gives us life in several different ways:

1. Creating us
2. Preserving us through the sun and rain
3. Saving us from sin by justifying us through faith in Christ
4. Permitting us through faith to live in Christ and for Christ to live in us by the new creation[2]
5. Promising all that is to come for those in Christ: resurrection and the new heaven and earth[3]

FOR LIFE JESUS DOESN'T WANT US TO MISS WHAT HE DID

When we see books on the bestseller list, we never see how any of these titles (no matter how amazing they seem) compare to the Holy Bible. There is a reason for this. If the comparison were shown, it would be instantly evident that no other book comes close to the worldwide dissemination of God's word.

It is no coincidence. The book that presents life to all people because God loves all people, God wants all people to have access to. And in this book, this holy book, this revelation from the God who is there, is the single most vital pivotal event in human history that proclaims that death is not the end. Not only this, but neither do we become a collective blob or change identities altogether.[4] That event was and is the event of the resurrection of the Lord Jesus Christ.

The accounting of it, therefore, is not in accord with the characteristics of mythology, but in accord with the signposts of real people in real places witnessing with their real eyes and touching with their real hands the real God who was there in the real flesh *once dead, but then was alive again in real history.*

2. Stage three as described in chapter 1.
3. Stage four.
4. We shall consider transmigration of the soul later in this volume.

Previously in this book in the section on miracles, we looked at the "top-down" approach in which we considered the evidence in the cosmos for the existence of a Creator ("top" meaning that which is above us in the heavens). Now we have arrived at the other way of knowing the viability of miracles through the "bottom-up" approach[5]—"bottom-up" because we begin considering evidence for the miraculous on earth (which is below, or at "bottom" of, the God of the universe). The events that occurred here on earth with respect to the resurrection of Jesus Christ are backed up with extraordinary details—earthbound evidence—that can be intelligently investigated.

As we discussed in chapter 4, none of this is about "proving" anything, but with eyes wide open, we have yet another impressive resonance between Jesus Christ and the things of real life and real history. It is the "resonating" that the God who is there would use for good to awaken people to their needs. Thus, being aware of that need, we might receive the word of Christ and the gift of saving faith worked by the Holy Spirit. So, let us continue to know what God has done to garner the attention of the people to whom he gave, and desires to give even more, life to.

THE CHRIST, THE REAL CHRIST

The resurrection of the Lord Jesus Christ cannot be considered apart from knowing exactly what Jesus said of himself. This is important because his signs were for the verification and confirmation of his words.

Jesus taught of his own divinity. In Mark 14:62, in front of the high priest, Jesus called himself "the Son of Man," who is the One with authority to judge all people as only God has. At this, the high priest acknowledged Jesus' meaning as he tore his garments, accusing him of blasphemy because he was calling himself God.

In Luke 5:20–24 (paralleled in Matt 9 and Mark 2), Jesus announced to the paralytic, "Man, your sins are forgiven you" (Luke 5:20). There is immediate pushback by the scribes and Pharisees who heard this: "Who can forgive sins but God alone?" (Luke 5:21). *Exactly!* And then—again for good measure—Jesus backs up his divine authority by commanding the paralytic to "rise and walk" (Luke 5:24), which is precisely what the paralytic did.

---

5. Again, with thanks to one of my former professors at Biola University, La Mirada, Douglas Geivett, ca. 1999–2002.

John 8:56–59 is astoundingly clear on this subject of Christ's self-claim:

> [He said to the Jews,] "Your father Abraham rejoiced that he would see my day. He saw it and was glad." So the Jews said to him, "You are not yet fifty years old, and have you seen Abraham?" Jesus said to them, "Truly, truly, I say to you, before Abraham was, I am." So they picked up stones to throw at him, but Jesus hid himself and went out of the temple.

When reading this section of John 8, it is difficult not to recall the words in Exodus when God revealed his name to Moses, "God said to Moses, 'I AM WHO I AM,' And he said, 'Say this to the people of Israel: 'I AM has sent me to you''" (Exod 3:14). And then Jesus comes along only two thousand years after Abraham was on earth and says to the Jews, "Truly, truly, I say to you, before Abraham was, I am" (John 8:58). And once again, there is no doubt that his opponents understood precisely what he had said and what he meant. That is why they picked up stones to throw at him (John 8:59). They just heard the thirty-something-year-old Jesus call himself God, the "I AM."

There is no question that Jesus claimed divinity in the above gospel accounts, but there is also testimony of his divinity in other New Testament references.[6] This same One so vividly identified also said he would raise himself from death (John 2:19, 21). And the event of his resurrection was so important, he would ensure people would be able to attest to it.

EYEWITNESSES EVERYWHERE

If a person ever wanted to make themselves look like a complete fool, then they could tell a lie and claim that other people witnessed what they were deceptively reporting. That way, anyone who heard their claims could then consult the others whom the liar said were witnesses. After such consultation, the liar's bluff would be thoroughly called.

---

6. For example: "To them belong the patriarchs, and from their race, according to the flesh, is the Christ, who is God over all, blessed forever. Amen" (Rom 9:5); "For by him all things were created, in heaven and on earth, visible and invisible, whether thrones or dominions or rulers or authorities—all things were created through him and for him" (Col 1:16); "But in these last days he has spoken to us by his Son, whom he appointed heir of all things, through whom also he created the world. He is the radiance of the glory of God and the exact imprint of his nature, and he upholds the universe by the word of his power" (Heb 1:2–3); and when Jesus says of himself, "I am the Alpha and the Omega, the first and the last, the beginning and the end" (Rev 22:13).

Otherwise, when eyewitnesses are involved, watch out. Now you're working with the dynamite of truth. It is also important to note that when we speak of eyewitnesses, we are indeed referring to the plural: *many* eyewitnesses, with the assurance that there is no such thing as mass hallucinations. It is one thing for a person to see a pink flying tiger drinking a Mai Tai, but it is another thing for such a vision to be seen by many people at the same time and place. Such a circumstance would no longer qualify as a hallucination, and we would have to alert the authorities about an interesting alien invasion taking place.

The resurrection of Jesus Christ is recorded by all four gospels and verified by the rest of the New Testament. In those Gospel accounts Jesus appeared to many:

1. Mary Magdalene (John 20:16, Mark 16:9), which is doubly significant in that Jesus honors a *woman* to see him first, even before the disciples, but truthful records don't succumb to cultural preferences
2. A group of other women returning from his tomb (Matt 28:9)
3. Simon Peter (Luke 24:34, 1 Cor 15:5)
4. Two disciples on the road to Emmaus (Luke 24:31, Mark 16:12)
5. Ten of the original disciples, with Thomas absent (John 20:19, Luke 24:36)
6. Eleven of the original disciples with Thomas present (John 20:26, Mark 16:14, 1 Cor 15:5)
7. Seven of the original disciples fishing at the sea of Tiberius (John 21:7)
8. The eleven original disciples at a mountain in Galilee (Matt 28:17)

In addition, the rest of the New Testament records Jesus Christ appearing to even more people:

9. Over five hundred "brethren" or fellow believers (1 Cor 15:6)
10. James, Jesus' brother (1 Cor 15:7)
11. At least the eleven apostles at his ascension (Acts 1:6)
12. Saul/Paul the apostle to the gentiles (Acts 9:5, 22:8; 1 Cor 15:8)

Gary R. Habermas and Michael R. Licona write,

> Sources that cannot be ignored are the Gospels themselves. No matter how skeptical the critic might be concerning the Gospels,

it is well-accepted that all four gospels (i.e., Matthew, Mark, Luke/Acts, John) were written during the first century. Each gospel attests to the resurrection of Jesus, and Acts is the sequel to the third gospel, Luke. This means that four accounts were written within seventy years of Jesus at the latest, reporting the disciples' claims that Jesus rose from the dead.[7]

The sheer number of historical details in respect to the resurrection put the eyewitnesses in the setting and context for being vetted by the most vehement opponents to Jesus Christ. The Roman governor overseeing the events was well known, the location crystal clear, and the details of Christ's burial were known to Christians, Jews, and Romans alike. John Warwick Montgomery puts this in historical perspective:

> Out of the first century A.D., when the Resurrection, if untrue, could have been easily disproved by anyone who took the trouble to talk with those who had been present in Jerusalem during the Passover week of 33, *no contrary historical evidence has come*; instead, during that century the number of conversions to Christianity increased by geometric progression, the influence of the Gospel story spreading out of Jerusalem like a gigantic web. If Christ did not rise as He promised, how can we rationally explain this lack of negative evidence and number of conversions?[8]

NOT JUST "E" FOR EYEWITNESS, BUT "E" FOR EARLY

Gary R. Habermas presents the critical quality of the two "E's" in respect to analyzing the resurrection of Jesus Christ.[9] The *eyewitness* (the first "E") reports are *early* (the second "E") in respect to their closeness to the time in history of the death, burial, and resurrection of the Lord Jesus Christ.

Habermas writes, "The closer the time between the event and testimony about it, the more reliable the witness, since there is less time for exaggeration, and even legend, to creep into the account."[10] We have already commented on the time of the gospels above, but the early time consideration becomes even more impressive in respect to the apostle Paul.

---

7. Habermas and Licona, *Case for the Resurrection*, 53.
8. Montgomery, "Quest for Absolutes," 7–8.
9. Habermas, "Jesus and the Resurrection."
10. Habermas and Licona, *Case for the Resurrection*, 39.

First Corinthians was written around AD 54–57, which was only about twenty-five years after the resurrection of Christ, but in 1 Cor 15:1–2, Saint Paul writes that he had already preached the gospel, including the message of Christ's resurrection, *prior* to his writing of 1 Corinthians. In addition, Saint Paul goes even further back into time about his knowledge of the resurrection of Christ by saying that this gospel, including the resurrection, was something he *received* (v. 3).[11]

When did Saint Paul receive this gospel? And recall, we are not counting the fact that Saint Paul reported on his own sighting of Christ on the road to Damascus. Here we are considering the historical record via oral tradition, *the* record of the people and culture at the time that was not from himself. It is most likely that Saint Paul received the gospel, including the knowledge of the resurrection of Christ, when he stayed in Jerusalem three years after his conversion (Gal 1:18).

How does this translate in terms of how close we come to the actual resurrection of Christ? Answer: the timing of Paul's knowledge would be *extremely* close to the event, as in three to five years after Jesus was crucified.[12] The implications are scintillating as Saint Paul had received and began to preach the resurrection of Jesus amid many enemies of the gospel, people who had been in and around Jerusalem at the time of Christ. The implication is massively important: there is no room for legend or myth in such a timeline.

EMPTY TOMB AND CHANGED LIVES

There are two other corresponding facts that should not be ignored. The first is that the tomb in which Jesus of Nazareth was buried was found empty after he was buried in it a few days before (in Jewish reckoning of days). This fact was known by just about everyone: it was known by the Romans, the Jews, and the Christians.

The moment one comes face-to-face with this fact, there are only so many places one can go with what happened to the body of Jesus Christ. Natural explanations can include (1) Christ's disciples stole his body, (2) authorities hid his body, (3) Christ merely "swooned" and did not die (known

---

11. Habermas, "Jesus and the Resurrection."
12. Habermas, "Jesus and the Resurrection."

as the swoon theory), (4) the disciples hatched the Passover Plot (explained below), or 5) Jesus was an alien.[13] Montgomery surveys the possibilities:

> If the body of the crucified Jesus naturally left the tomb, how did it leave? Not by its own accord, for Jesus was unquestionably dead. Not through the efforts of the Jewish religious leaders or the Romans, for they had placed a guard at the tomb for the express purpose for keeping the body there. Not Jesus' followers, for to perform such an act would have been to deny the principles of truth upon which their later lives were predicated, and which they preached until killed for their convictions. If Jesus did not rise from the dead, what happened to His body in the city teeming with the Passover crowd, a great number of whom had been members of the mob which required us to admit the truth of the Resurrection; probability, which is the criterion of truth of the historian, must rule over any *a priori* considerations in making of historical judgments. Can miracles occur? History and not philosophy must answer this question.[14]

The historical details support the miraculous. With their leader gone and their spirits defeated while they hid after Christ's crucifixion (John 20), the last thing the disciples would have done was steal their Savior's body. Not only would such a devious action completely contradict everything he had taught them, but they would have suffered every persecution to the extent of martyrdom (except John) for a lie. In the other words, if they had merely stolen the body of Christ, they would not have endured such persecution based on their testimony to the resurrection.

For the enemies of Christ to hide Christ's body would be to perpetuate the controversy and trouble they had every reason to avoid. Pontius Pilate gave into the demands of the crowd to crucify Christ to avoid chaos. Thus, he was not about to reignite it after Christ was buried. As for the Jews doing this, that would be for them to ask to perpetuate the very "rumor"—that Christ was raised—that they sought to dispel.

The swoon theory is that Jesus didn't die on the cross and was therefore buried alive. Then, he snapped out of unconsciousness and somehow made his way out of the sealed tomb from the inside. The idea is beyond ludicrous. Suffice it to say again that the Romans were expert executioners,

---

13. For this list, I am indebted to Dr. Craig Hazen's teaching during my time at Biola University.

14. Montgomery, "Quest for Absolutes," 7–8.

and further, no one was going to be impressed by a "risen" Christ who was marred and weak beyond words.

The Passover Plot is the creative idea that Jesus and his disciples had devised a plan of deception (again, going against everything Jesus taught). The plan was that he would feign death, but the plan got out of hand, and he actually died (something not anticipated). To compensate, the disciples found someone to impersonate Jesus, or perhaps even an unknown twin was discovered to appear as the resurrected Jesus. This idea does not dignify further commentary.

The last logical possibility in the realm of natural explanations is that Jesus was an alien. It just so happens that this idea fits all the historical data. It would account for the empty tomb, the fact that the disciples absolutely believed they had seen and touched Christ, the fact that these disciples were transformed into bold proclaimers of Jesus willing to die for the gospel, and that the legitimacy of these circumstances led to the explosive growth of the Christian church including the incalculable conversions such as that of James the brother of Christ who had been a skeptic, and Paul who had formerly persecuted Christians. The problem with the alien hypothesis is that it contradicts the teaching of Christ about his actual humanity.

There is one *other* explanation that fits all the historical data—namely, Jesus was who he said he was and he truly rose from the dead.

God, the real God, does not need to defend himself, and he is not out to try to impress people, but what he *does* desire is that people be saved and come to the knowledge of the truth (1 Tim 2:4). He puts forth resonating truth that people might seek him and, when they do, find him. Through the resurrection of Christ, God made a splash in human history and has supplied a banner for answering the question "Where is God?" He is in his Son, Jesus Christ, who came into our world to be born, to live, to die, and to rise from death so that we might know God. And because he rose, he is alive right now so that we can confidently know that he was and is the death of death. That is, for those who trust in him, death will not—it cannot—have the last word. And Jesus has made another promise: he is coming again. To this promise, we now turn.

PART II | SECOND ARTICLE OF THE CREED

CHAPTER 7 DISCUSSION GUIDE: CONTENDING FOR JESUS, THE DEATH OF DEATH

UNCOVER INFORMATION

1. What is a miracle?
2. When have miracles occurred in human history?
3. According to Luther, who is the "devil" of the devil?
4. What has God designed us to desire, even crave?
5. How many resurrection appearances of Christ are recorded in Scripture?

DISCOVER MEANING

1. Why didn't Jesus put on a show of miracles for Herod?
2. Why were the miracles of Christ in alignment with what he preached? What does this teach us about the purpose of biblical miracles?
3. How consistent is the miracle of creation, with God using nothing, complementary to God raising us from dust? Discuss.
4. Why did Christ give testimony about himself the way he did?
5. What is the significance of the two "E's" for biblical reliability and evidence for Christ's bodily resurrection?

EXPLORE IMPLICATIONS

1. If Christ is merely a man, what of his resurrection?
2. What is the biblical significance of highlighting the faith of the Syrophoenician woman and the Roman centurion? Connect their example to our faith in Christ's resurrection.
3. Why is it important that Scripture records not only the Father and the Holy Spirit raising Christ, but also that Christ raised himself?
4. Why would God give us so many examples of giving, sustaining, and promising life to us? How should the baptized respond?

5. How much stock do we put into eyewitness testimony to track human history? Does it surprise you that the saving faith employs this characteristic as well? Why or why not?

8

Contending for Jesus, the Keeper of Promises Coming Again

"I believe in God . . . and in Jesus Christ. . . .
From [heaven] he will come to judge the living and the dead."

JESUS KEEPS HIS PREDICTIONS AND PROMISES

Jesus speaks the truth. He does not lie. Of course, this is what we would expect from God. This makes his promises especially important to people. He is not like the rest of us. Sometimes we make promises with the best of intentions, but then life comes to visit, whipping up circumstances we could have never predicted. As a result, most people have experience with broken promises. Jesus, however, never breaks his promises.

God in the flesh clearly told his disciples that he was going to be crucified and then be raised from death, not once, not twice, but on three separate occasions.

First in Matt 16:21–26, Mark 8:31–37, and Luke 9:22:25, which include the words, "From that time Jesus began to show his disciples that he must go to Jerusalem and suffer many things from the elders and chief priests and scribes, and be killed, and on the third day be raised" (Matt 16:21).

Second in Matt 17:22–23, Mark 9:30–32, and Luke 9:43b–45 which include the words, "For he was teaching his disciples, saying to them, 'The

Son of Man is going to be delivered into the hands of men, and they will kill him. And when he is killed, after three days he will rise'" (Mark 9:31).

Third in Matt 20:17-19, Mark 10:32-34, and Luke 18:31-34 which include the words, "And taking the twelve, he said to them, 'See, we are going up to Jerusalem, and everything that is written about the Son of Man by the prophets will be accomplished. For he will be delivered over to the Gentiles and will be mocked and shamefully treated and spit upon. And after flogging him, they will kill him, and on the third day he will rise'" (Luke 18:32-33).

The implications of such a prediction cannot be overestimated. A Jewish man could not have claimed control over Roman judicial proceedings. Of course, as Jesus was and is the Godman, he was also able to speak amazing words to Pilate: "You would have no authority over me at all unless it had been given you from above" (John 19:11). From a human perspective, how could a man dictate what Pilate was going to do? Even this in respect to Christ's death, however, pales in comparison to the rest of Jesus' prediction.

What mere man could say in such clear terms that after his crucifixion, he would rise from the dead? And did you notice the exactness of Christ's prediction in the Scriptures quoted above? That he will "on the third day be raised" (Matt 16:21); "after three days he will rise" (Mark 9:31); and "on the third day he will rise" (Luke 18:33). His precise predictions came to pass. What he said would happen, happened.

But stepping away from his own person, he made another staggering prediction in respect to the most holy place of the Jews. Herod the Great had commenced an incredible remodeling project for the temple that already had been going on for forty-six years, mentioned in Holy Scripture when Jesus spoke of his own temple, his body (John 2:20).

Jesus told his disciples what was going to happen to the magnificent temple in Jerusalem: "Jesus left the temple and was going away, when his disciples came to point out to him the buildings of the temple. But he answered them, 'You see all these, do you not? Truly, I say to you, there will not be left here one stone upon another that will not be thrown down'" (Matt 24:1-2). His words are reinforced in Mark's gospel (Mark 13:1-2), as well as Luke's gospel (Luke 21:5-6).

As he made this startling prediction of what would eventually occur (and about forty years after he said it would happen, it did), he elaborated upon the coming destruction in vivid detail. All of it would come to pass as he said it would. No one could imagine it occurring, but he knew.

But Jesus made another promise-prediction which has been fulfilled and continues to be fulfilled not just for mere decades, but for millennia.

Peter, and the other apostles faithful to their risen Lord's commission, preached the gospel with the signs from God that accompanied them; he had earned the anger and angst of the religious authorities (Acts 5). These authorities had Peter and the other apostles brought to them: "And when they had brought them, they set them before the council. And the high priest questioned them, saying, 'We strictly charged you not to teach in this name, yet here you have filled Jerusalem with your teaching, and you intend to bring this man's blood upon us.' But Peter and the apostles answered, 'We must obey God rather than men'" (Acts 5:27–29).

The sacred text goes on to tell us that the council was enraged and wanted to kill them (Acts 5:33). But then a Pharisee among them named Gamaliel, a highly respected member of the council, gave orders for the apostles to be put outside that he might speak to the council. With the apostles no longer in his hearing, he spoke:

> Men of Israel, take care what you are about to do with these men. For before these days Theudas rose up, claiming to be somebody, and a number of men, about four hundred, joined him. He was killed, and all who followed him were dispersed and came to nothing. After him Judas the Galilean rose up in the days of the census and drew away some of the people after him. He too perished, and all who followed him were scattered. So in the present case I tell you, keep away from these men and let them alone, for if this plan or this undertaking is of man, it will fail; but if it is of God, you will not be able to overthrow them. You might even be found opposing God! (Acts 5:35–39)

What Jesus had predicted and promised was already in the book of Acts coming to fulfillment. The ministry Peter and the other apostles were conducting was not "of man" but was "of God." Jesus had said this would happen.

Jesus had once asked the disciples what they heard people saying about him. He asked them, "Who do people say that the Son of Man is?" They answered him by listing the most popular responses that had been floating around (e.g., that Christ was John the Baptist, Elijah, Jeremiah, or another prophet). Jesus then pinpointed his question to what *they* said about him: "But who do you say that I am?" (Matt 16:15). Peter gave an inspired and true answer: "You are the Christ, the Son of the living God" (Matt 16:16).

When Peter said this, Jesus affirmed him, stating that what he had just said had been revealed to him by God (Matt 16:17). And then Jesus said this:

> And I tell you, you are Peter, and on this rock I will build my church, and the gates of hell shall not prevail against it. (Matt 16:18)

Upon the confession that Jesus is the Christ (the long-awaited Messiah, the very Son of God, of the same essence as the Father), through this confession and apostolic ministry (Jesus' ministry on earth), Jesus said, "I will build my church." In that instance, Jesus had made a promise.

And build it he has. He has kept his promise. Christians should never get caught up in statistics. They never tell the whole story, but they are nevertheless relevant. Gamaliel said in the early first century that if what Peter and the other apostles were doing was from God, then anyone opposing their ministry would not be able to overthrow them. When Gamaliel said this, Pentecost had just occurred with the outpouring of the Holy Spirit, and it is recorded that "about three thousand souls" were added to the number of the first disciples of Christ (Acts 2:33, 41).

That is, at the time of Gamaliel's words about the sign of God's providential working (which would demonstrate the truthfulness of Jesus' promise), there were about three thousand Christians. Today, there are over two billion.

WHEN JESUS' PROMISES REALLY GET PERSONAL

Jesus' record of promise-keeping is impeccable. He said he would be crucified, and he was. He said he would rise on the third day, and he did. He said the temple would be destroyed, and it was. He said he would build his church, and he has. But he has also made another set of promises to his people:

- "For where two or three are gathered in my name, there am I among them" (Matt 18:20).
- "And behold, I am with you always, to the end of the age" (Matt 28:20b).
- "For he has said, 'I will never leave you nor forsake you'" (Heb 13:5).

This promise he also keeps. What is so difficult along life's path, however, is that we often do not want what life brings us. When this happens, it is easy for people—be it at stage two, as one without conversion to Christ, or even stage three, as one with conversion to Christ but still impacted by the sinful nature—to suspect or even complain that God has not been there during the times of our pain. But this perception does not mean Christ has broken his promise.

For example, he had made his promise never to leave very evident to Saint Stephen. He loved God and followed Christ. Stephen was faithful and upon the occasion of proclaiming the truth of God's word, the people who heard him were enraged (Acts 7:54). Stephen, however, full of the Holy Spirit, saw the glory of God and Jesus standing at the right hand of God (Acts 7:55–56). Those who rejected God rejected Stephen and began to stone him to death. The scene in Holy Scripture ends with these words: "And as they were stoning Stephen, he called out, 'Lord Jesus, receive my spirit.' And falling to his knees he cried out with a loud voice, 'Lord, do not hold this sin against them.' And when he had said this, he fell asleep'" (Acts 7:59–60).

From a worldly perspective, Christ did not keep his promise to Stephen, because he was stoned to death while being faithful to God. But this is the world's perspective, and it does not change the fact that Christ had positively kept his promise to Stephen. He had kept it so powerfully for him in fact, that Stephen was comforted in seeing the risen Christ in glory with his own eyes. Christ was with him so radiantly that being inspired by his presence—even while dying—Stephen prayed for those who were murdering him. Stephen knew full well that Jesus was keeping his promise to never leave him even through what the world could only perceive as a horrific moment in time.

This fact has not changed for God's people one iota. When we are in Christ, we are permitted to know crosses like our Savior, who knew *the* cross for the sins of the world. These crosses are not pleasant, but they are used by God to show us the way of faith in this world.[1] Christians are enabled to remain under their crosses through Christ's church that they might constantly receive Jesus himself through his word and Sacrament.[2] In this way, faith remains strong as we undoubtedly continue to experience the fulfillment of our Lord's promise to us to be with us always until the end of days.

---

1. About these crosses, I elaborated a great deal in *Faith That Shines*.
2. Something we shall elaborate upon in the next part of this volume.

UPON ANOTHER PROMISE OF JESUS, WE AWAIT

Christians contend for this Christ who keeps his promises. And it is not happenstance that so many of his promises were recorded so that people could see that there is someone who loves them and who will not break his word to them. This Christ has given another promise which Christians confess constantly in the creed: Jesus promised to come again.

Jesus' promise to come again is referred to in a very special way in Holy Scripture. Christians anticipate and are "waiting for our blessed hope, the appearing of the glory of our great God and Savior Jesus Christ" (Titus 2:13). The second coming of Jesus is *our blessed hope*.

This is an important designation to say the least. The second coming of the Lord Jesus Christ is not a threat to God's people but a glorious event to be yearned for. Thus, Jesus taught about how Christians should view this last day when he would be seen "coming in a cloud with power and great glory" (Luke 21:27). Jesus said, "Now when these things begin to take place, straighten up and raise your heads, because your redemption is drawing near" (Luke 21:28). To be able to raise one's head to see redemption coming is something describing the occasion for great joy, to put it mildly. It means not only that life will continue in a way that is better than life has ever been or otherwise could ever be, but it also means the cessation of all suffering and pain.

In the great book of Revelation, written in an apocalyptic writing style marked by symbolism, numerology, and figurative language, Saint John describes what is to come for the people of God. It will be a place in which there will be countless multitudes. In one instance in Revelation, a heavenly elder describes to the apostle in his glorious vision the gathering of people who received the redemption at Christ's second coming:

> These are the ones coming out of the great tribulation. They have washed their robes and made them white in the blood of the Lamb. Therefore they are before the throne of God, and serve him day and night in his temple; and he who sits on the throne will shelter them with his presence. They shall hunger no more, neither thirst anymore; the sun shall not strike them, nor any scorching heat. For the Lamb in the midst of the throne will be their shepherd, and he will guide them to springs of living water, and God will wipe away every tear from their eyes. (Rev 7:14–17)

The description of what is to come for the people of God includes the sympathetic mentioning of what they came through: "the great tribulation."

This is a reference to the hardship experienced while in the world that came upon God's children in many and various ways. Distinctions are important here because not all the suffering is the same.

God teaches his people, "If you are insulted for the name of Christ, you are blessed, because the Spirit of glory and of God rests upon you. But let none of you suffer as a murderer or a thief or an evildoer or as a meddler. Yet if anyone suffers as a Christian, let him not be ashamed, but let him glorify God in that name" (1 Pet 4:14–16).

People suffer for many reasons, but when God's people suffer for living as his people, seeking his righteousness, but get the world's smiting in return, this can make even the child of God wonder, "How long will I have to endure this?" God knows. This is why the blessed hope of the second coming of Christ is so important to the Christian.

The second coming of Jesus serves us to give us encouragement in the face of life's hardships. Jesus did not mince words to his first-century disciples (words that apply also to his twenty-first-century disciples), "In the world you will have tribulation. But take heart; I have overcome the world" (John 16:33b).

We wait for this promise of his second coming to be fulfilled, and again, with Jesus' track record for keeping promises, we know it will be.

It is appropriate in the meantime for the Christian not simply to wait, but also to desire for this day to come sooner than later. Still, we should understand that the reason the Lord has not yet come is because there is work to do here on earth before that last day.

While acknowledging that going to be the Lord is "far better" (Phil 1:23), Saint Paul also acknowledged that to be on earth meant "fruitful labor" (Phil 1:20). The fruitful labor for the Christian includes worshiping God, serving the neighbor, praying to the Lord, and witnessing to others about Christ. It is a labor the world desperately needs, and it is a labor that makes the life of the Christian not simply a life, but a mission and ministry. Thus, Christians live in a lively tension: they eagerly await the second coming of Christ, and they relish the fruitful labor the Lord has for them to do until he comes.

WHAT'S TAKING SO LONG?

Skeptics, however, feel more justified in their incredulity and incorrigibility because if God is truly the God who is there, what's taking so long? This mockery has gone on for a long time. Saint Peter addressed this:

> I am stirring up your sincere mind by way of reminder, that you should remember the predictions of the holy prophets and the commandment of the Lord and Savior through your apostles, knowing that first of all, that scoffers will come in the last days with scoffing, following their own sinful desires. They will say, "Where is the promise of his coming? For ever since the fathers fell asleep, all things are continuing as they were from the beginning of creation." For they deliberately overlook this fact, that the heavens existed long ago, and the earth was formed out of water and through water by the word of God, and that by means of these the world that then existed was deluged with water and perished. But by the same word the heavens and earth that now exist are stored up for fire, being kept until the day of judgment and destruction of the ungodly. But do not overlook this one fact, beloved, that with the Lord one day is as a thousand years, and a thousand years as one day. The Lord is not slow to fulfill his promise as some count slowness, but is patient toward you, not wishing that any should perish, but that all should reach repentance. (2 Pet 3:1b–9)

As a pastor ministering to the elderly, I have lost count of how many times I've heard God's people in their eighties, nineties, and even past the century mark say in one way or another, "Time flies by," and "It seemed like yesterday when . . ." and I have been reminded in my own experience how true this is. Most people can probably relate to this. Time is also God's creation, and he is not disturbed by it. He simply tells us that our time is fleeting and that he gives more time that we "should reach repentance." The psalmist did not hold back this truth:

> O Lord, make me know my end and what is the measure of my days; let me know how fleeting I am! Behold, you have made my days a few handbreadths, and my lifetime is as nothing before you. Surely all mankind stands as a mere breath! (Ps 39:4–5)

Saint James in the New Testament echoes the psalmist from the Old Testament: "Yet you do not know what tomorrow will bring. What is your life? For you are a mist that appears for a little time and then vanishes" (Jas 4:14).

It is, therefore, quite true that time is rather relative (and Einstein would agree). If it seems that God is taking a long time to fulfill the promise of Christ's coming, then think again. In truth, time is flying by, and in the meantime, God is being patient and gracious, giving people time to come to faith in Jesus.

CONTENDING FOR THE TRUTH OF CHRIST'S SECOND COMING

As God's people wait for the blessed hope, the church must be on guard against strange ideas about the second coming of Christ. It seems that there is no promise of Christ that has not been doubted and resisted. Peter resisted Christ's prediction that he was going to Jerusalem to be killed (Matt 16:22). The world has doubted the fulfillment of the promised resurrection ever since it was predicted by Christ. And who would have thought that his prediction of the temple's destruction would come to pass? As for the knowledge that God does not forsake us through our tribulations, what person has not doubted, at best, and turned away from God to curse him, at worst? This happened with Job himself when his wife encouraged him to curse God in his misery and die (Job 2:9).

In the same way, people not only doubt and deny the second coming of Christ, but even within Christendom, it is diluted in terrible ways. One of those wrong approaches to Christ's teaching about his second coming is when it is used for fearmongering. This teaching is called "dispensationalism," which teaches that God has related to his people through the ages in different ways. This is true to the extent that dispensationalism teaches that God's salvation toward his people is different depending on the dispensation, epoch, or era (or simply, the unique time in history) in which they lived (though many dispensationalists would deny this).

The general concept of dispensationalism is nothing new. One of the most famous early dispensationalists was Joachim of Fiore (Joachim of Flore, ca. 1132–1202). He is famously known for dividing history corresponding to the three persons of the Holy Trinity so that there is an age of the Father, an age of the Son, and an age of the Holy Spirit.

Present-day dispensationalism, however, was developed by John Nelson Darby (1800–1882). His system goes beyond only three dispensations, to seven. He was a religious leader in Britain and a founder of the Plymouth Brethren sect. It was his unique teaching, however, that made him famous.

What Darby offered was not only a highly systematic schema for organizing history, but an approach to Holy Scripture that aimed to reveal the mystery of God's word with fixed categories, complicated arithmetic, and predictions. It is hard to imagine a more impressive form of dispensationalism.

The general descriptions provided by Darby for his seven dispensations have proven steady, but since the early nineteenth century, there have been many variations. It's popularity and growth in America was perpetuated by C. I. Scofield, who wrote the bestselling annotated *Scofield Reference Bible* on dispensationalism first released in 1909. This spilled over into the work of Hal Lindsey, whose book *The Late Great Planet Earth* was the bestselling book in the 1970s of *any* genre. The teaching can also be seen in the publications of Tim LaHaye and Jerry Jenkins of the *Left Behind* novels, which sold almost eighty million copies. Here we see a more current description of the seven dispensations into the twenty-first century:

The First:	Innocence (Creation)
The Second:	Conscience (The Fall)
The Third:	Human Government (Flood)
The Fourth:	Promise (Tower of Babel)
The Fifth:	Law (Exodus)
The Sixth:	Church Age (Israel Dispersed)
The Seventh:	Millennial Reign[3]

The system is contrary to the basic teaching of the Christian church for two millennia and is a dangerous teaching, but why so?

1. It confuses the singular Messiah/Christ and salvation that comes through faith in him from Genesis through Revelation.
2. A peculiar feature of the teaching insists that the temple in Jerusalem be rebuilt, which is an example of point 1. This teaching produces confusion about the final atoning sacrifice of the Lord Jesus Christ.
3. It confuses the new Israel (God's people) with the political Israel of the twenty-first century. Instead of faith in Jesus, it connects the new Israel with the political state of Israel.

---

3. LaHaye and Ice, *Charting the End Times*, 83.

4. It introduces a relatively recent understanding of the "rapture." This unbiblical version of the "rapture" is by a secret and invisible coming of Christ that would remove all Christians on earth. However, this teaching had always been understood as occurring concurrently with the second coming of Christ on the last day (1 Thess 4:17).

5. It treats the twenty-one judgments in the book of Revelation as still coming in the future by understanding them in a wooden literalistic fashion while by-passing the unique genre of Revelation.

6. It uses point 5 as part of its wrong teaching of a seven-year tribulation coming after their unbiblical "rapture." This is a prime example of fearmongering: "Don't be left behind and suffer the terrible calamities of the tribulation."

7. It offers a second-chance theology so that people who put off believing in Jesus the first time around and find themselves "left behind" during the tribulation may finally come to saving faith.

8. It embarrassingly uses the words "left behind" in the exact opposite way as presented in Holy Scripture. When these words are used in the New Testament, those who are "left behind" are preserved and saved, while those "taken" are those who are condemned.

9. It teaches that the devil has not yet been bound by God and that he still dominates the world. Biblical Christianity confesses that when Jesus said from the cross, "It is finished" (John 19:30), he fulfilled the prophecy of Gen 3:15. This predicted that he would crush Satan's head—that is, utterly defeat him. Thus, in Matt 28:18, Jesus declared, "All authority in heaven and on earth has been given to me." And Jesus also said, "I saw Satan fall like lightning from heaven" (Luke 10:18). This is why he can instruct his followers, "Resist the devil, and he will flee from you" (Jas 4:7).

10. It teaches a wooden literalistic thousand-year reign of Christ on the earth after their wrong tribulation. This misses the reality of Christ reigning through his church today, not through political power but by the power of his grace, word, and sacraments to deliver people from sin, death, and the devil. The thousand years are symbolic for the perfect time of Christ's church before his second coming on the last day.[4]

---

4. Espinosa, "Apocalyptic Anxiety." This ten-point summary was uniquely written for this present volume, but represents a short summary of my doctoral research which

In the final analysis, for two millennia the church has properly taught about Christ's second coming and the attending events of the last day. These include the resurrection of all people from the dead (1 Cor 15), the one and only rapture of God's people to the right hand of Christ in the air (1 Thess 4:17), the judgment of all people before Christ (Matt 25), and the resultant assignment to eternal life or eternal reprobation (Rev 21). But relatively recently in time, dispensationalism came to cause confusion that this teaching is *the* teaching of the Christian church and of Jesus. Nothing could be further from the truth.

The teaching, however, is also capable of producing a soulish void: since dispensationalism also negates the Sacraments of Jesus Christ, the adherent must look for ways to feel confident that they are true believers. But this is one reason why the Sacraments were given. When the Sacraments are rejected, however, something must fill the void, and often dispensationalism reverts to political activism. In this way, many people without Christ are turned away from Christ because they see Christianity become another version of political power. However, Jesus said more than once, "My Kingdom is not of this world" (John 18:36).

FEARMONGERING IS ONE THING, BUT A LOVING WARNING IS SOMETHING ELSE

Finally, we must consider that the creed says that at his second coming, the Lord Jesus Christ will *judge*. What is he going to judge? He will judge whether people trusted in the mercy of the true God in and through Christ, or whether they trusted in something else to deal with that universal sense of off-ness and need for something beyond themselves.

Recall the discussion above on the points on the mathematical line, be it spanning across the universe or an inch on a ruler, there is a sense in which eternity is in all people as well. The word of God states, "He has made everything beautiful in its time. Also, he has put eternity into man's heart" (Eccl 3:11). The natural knowledge of God is in the hearts of all people. The eternal God is there and everyone, if they are honest, know deep in their hearts that they need him.

The judgment is not an event in which God treats people maliciously. Not at all; it is rather an acknowledgement of what each person has chosen:

---

also considered dispensationalism's influence both upon American politics and popular American Christianity's idea of Christian sanctification.

to do it on their own, or to do it with the grace of their Creator and Savior. We will look more closely at this situation in the coming section and especially in the last chapter of this volume. It is time now to consider the third and last part of the creed.

CHAPTER 8 DISCUSSION GUIDE: CONTENDING FOR JESUS, THE KEEPER OF PROMISES COMING AGAIN

UNCOVER INFORMATION

1. What promises that Jesus made during his earthly ministry have already occurred?
2. What is the very personal promise Jesus has made to every Christian?
3. What is the second coming of Christ called in the Bible?
4. What is the proper understanding of the "great tribulation"?
5. What is John Nelson Dary known for?

DISCOVER MEANING

1. In your own words, what did Gamaliel tell the council about the apostles?
2. Review the personal promises of Christ to his people. How can these be reconciled with what happened to Saint Stephen?
3. Why does the Lord Jesus Christ instruct Christians to "raise [their] heads" at his glorious second coming?
4. What is the "living tension" Christians live in as they await their death and/or the last day?
5. Please see the ten dangerous teachings of dispensationalism. Consider point 4. What are the two major understandings of "rapture" from 1 Thess 4:17?

EXPLORE IMPLICATIONS

1. Why is it important to differentiate between the second coming of Christ viewed as a day of joy instead of a day of fear?
2. List three of the prophetic predictions of Jesus that have come to pass. How does Jesus' record of accuracy give confidence about his second coming?
3. How does 2 Pet 3:1b–9 help the Christian answer the question, "What is taking Christ so long?"
4. What dangers are inherent in dispensationalism?
5. What should people do in light of the Scriptures teaching that Jesus will judge on the last day?

PART III

Contending for the Faith According to the Third Article of the Creed

9

Contending for the Holy Christian Church

> "I believe in God, . . . the Holy Spirit, **the holy Christian church, the communion of saints** . . ."

HOW CAN THE CHURCH BE FOUND?

The true church is the persecuted church. As a result, she isn't impressive to the world. And the last thing the world wants is to be like Jesus. To the world, his way is too bleak. After all, he bore a cross; who wants to follow *that*? But this is exactly what he calls his people to: "If anyone would come after me, let him deny himself and take up his cross and follow me" (Matt 16:24).

What happened to Jesus happens to his church, and what happens to his church, even to this day, happens to Jesus. Jesus taught his disciples, "'A servant is not greater than his master.' If they persecuted me, they will also persecute you" (John 15:20). When Saul of Tarsus was not yet the transformed apostle Paul, Jesus confronted him on the Damascus road and asked him, "Saul, Saul, why are you persecuting me?" (Acts 9:4). Christ had already risen from death, but his communion with his church was such that their persecution was his. That is how much Jesus identifies with his church and how much his church identifies with him. The stunned and bewildered Saint Paul responded, "Who are you, Lord?" The God who is there replied, "I am Jesus, whom you are persecuting" (Acts 9:5).

What is more, this church characterized by crosses does not emit the best marketing to the world either. She just isn't all that impressive. As the individual believer still battles within himself (stage three), the church on earth—though she is completely holy in Christ—is still beleaguered in her struggle against sin, the world, and the devil. Thus, as long as she abides on earth, she is the church militant.[1]

When Saint Paul wrote to the church in Corinth, this congregation was inundated with troubles: they were riddled with jealousy and strife (1 Cor 3:3), infected by extreme sexual immorality within their communion (1 Cor 5:1), marked by mockery within their fellowship as they engaged in lawsuits against one another before unbelievers (1 Cor 6:1–8), and they were hampered by division among themselves which denigrated their worship (1 Cor 11:17–22).

The seeming inadequacies of Christ's people under their crosses continue to elicit criticisms of a culture ready to take its potshots at the church. All her past failures and current weaknesses are recalled and magnified with gladness by the world that is happy to welcome her demise.

The church plagued with weaknesses, however, has another side. People simply commit glaring *non sequiturs* (conclusions which do not logically follow stated premises) all the time when it comes to the church. Namely, just because Christ suffered does not disprove his deity. Similarly, just because the church is plagued by weaknesses, this does not mean she is not one with God in the mystical communion she enjoys with Christ. Shortcomings do not eliminate what is good and true.[2]

But how can the true church be found in this world? Christians need to know the current signs the Holy Spirit provides for all the world to see. These are the signs of God in the world today in the twenty-first century that say, "Here is where Christ dwells!" There are real signs, identifiable marks and unmistakable empirical signposts. They are priceless and give the baptized into Christ comfort, peace, and guidance in the world today. What are these marks of the church?

In his 1539 treatise *On the Councils and the Church*, Luther taught—with so many distractions in the world swirling about—exactly where Christ's church is found. And in finding the church, then the God who is there is also found. Luther listed seven marks of the true church, these are

---

1. Not because she is against people but because people in the world are against her.
2. See my extended apologetic in view of the criticisms of Yuval Noah Harari which I address in Espinosa, *Faith That Engages*.

important to know because just as there are false Christians and false revelations or "words" of God, there are also false "churches." Luther elaborated,

> Now when the devil saw that God built such a holy church, he was not idle, and erected his chapel beside it, larger than God's temple. This is how he did it: he noticed that God utilized outward things, like baptism, word, sacrament, keys, etc., whereby he sanctified his church. And since the devil is always God's ape, trying to imitate all God's things and to improve on them, he also tried his luck with external things purported to make man holy—just as he tries with rainmakers, sorcerers, exorcists of devils, etc. He even has the Lord's Prayer recited and the gospel read over them to make it appear a great holy possession.[3]

It is therefore crucial that the true church be found in accord with its proper marks. All aping and deception will then be eliminated so that we might never confuse God's church for Satan's chapel. Indeed, the Father of Lies is very religious, but everything he does is counterfeit. Thank God that there is a litmus test for what is true. Let us see about these seven marks of the true church.

THE WORD

In chapter 5 we discussed the historical reliability of the word of God and what makes it unique from the standpoint of its integrity as a trustworthy special revelation of God to humanity. But now we are looking at the word as a mark pointing to the integrity of something else—namely, the true church. In this church, the word of God is given free rein to do what God intends for it to do in the twenty-first century.

In the church, the Holy Spirit is active in working through the word of God to make disciples of Christ. A "disciple" is a hearer or learner of Christ's teaching, and that hearing of Christ's word can lead a person to experience the Spirit of God forging faith in their heart. Then, such a "hearer" does more than just hear; they are led to put into practice what they have learned by actively following Christ and doing "good works, which God prepared beforehand, that [his people] should walk in them" (Eph 2:10). This entire life, however, begins with the word of Christ. Jesus himself said, "If you abide in my word, you are truly my disciples" (John 8:31).

---

3. Luther, *Church and Ministry*, 167–68.

Part III | Third Article of the Creed

This is the great sign of the Holy Spirit working today: transforming the real lives of real people to be devout in the word of Christ. In this way, people are made privy to a treasure on earth. With this insight about the word of God, the child of God can relate to Jeremiah the prophet: "Your words were found, and I ate them, and your words became to me a joy and the delight of my heart, for I am called by your name O Lord, God of hosts" (Jer 15:16).

The word of God, also known as God's "sacred writings"—as Saint Paul taught—can make one "wise for salvation through faith in Christ Jesus" (2 Tim 3:15), be trained for righteousness (2 Tim 3:16), and make the man of God "complete, equipped for every good work" (2 Tim 3:17).

These are the signs that matter: that within the church, the Spirit of the Living God works through the word of Christ to change the lives of people. These are the signs God has given us today. For this reason, Luther prayed that he would not receive extraordinary phenomena from God, but instead he prayed to receive the clarity of the word of Christ.

> I have often stated that at the beginning of my cause I always asked the Lord not to send me dreams, visions, or angels. For many fanatical spirits attacked me, one of whom boasted of dreams, another of visions, and another of revelations with which they were striving to instruct me. But I replied that I was not seeking such revelations and that if any were offered, I would put no trust in them. And I prayed ardently to God that He might give me the sure meaning and understanding of Holy Scripture. For if I have the Word, I know that I am proceeding on the right way and cannot easily be deceived or go wrong.[4]

There is nothing to be cherished more than the knowledge of where God has promised to be found: in his church, where the word of Christ is freely given to all who seek him. In the meantime, the child of God is aware of the aping of the evil one. He, too, builds a "holy place" (the "chapel" Luther mentioned), with a false "word," marked with counterfeit signs and wonders, and with servants who masquerade as if belonging to Christ but who serve only themselves.

If anyone offers a different "word," then the church is no longer present. And no matter the spectacle that might be presented, we ought to remind ourselves of what is needed instead of what tries to ignite man's infatuation with the latest buzz.

---

4. Luther, *Genesis*, 119–20.

Jesus once told Martha about what her sister, Mary, had chosen when she chose to sit at Jesus' feet to hear his word and to learn from him: "Martha, Martha, you are anxious and troubled about many things, but one thing is necessary. Mary has chosen the good portion [receiving his word], which will not be taken away from her" (Luke 10:41–42). God's church is marked by the "good portion" and the "one thing necessary"—namely, the word of Christ.

This first mark of the church, therefore, is an empirically audible word. There is a broadcast, which takes place to reach the ears, hearts, and minds of people on earth.

HOLY BAPTISM

Luther taught in the *Small Catechism*, "Baptism is not just plain water, but it is the water included in God's command and combined with God's word."[5] But if Holy Baptism already contains the first mark of the church, the word, then why treat Holy Baptism as a separate mark of the church? It might help to consider an analogy.

In holy matrimony, the couple speaks vows. That is, they speak words to express their sacred oath, and through their speaking of sacred words, they are pronounced husband and wife. And yet, there is still another aspect to their binding as they become one in the marital union: they exchange rings.

The rings in holy matrimony are a kind of visible seal or sign that what has been spoken has now taken effect. The husband and wife who bear the rings are now one in the eyes of God. God says of them who are now bound, "What therefore God has joined together, let not man separate" (Matt 19:6b).

Holy Baptism is like the wedding band, but it surpasses the wedding band in that it is no mere symbol, but while containing the word of Christ, it works a "seal" upon the one who is baptized. Not only does Holy Baptism give the Holy Spirit who himself is a seal for the child of God (Eph 1:13, 4:30; 2 Cor 1:21–22) but itself unites the baptized with Christ.

Saint Paul writes, "Do you not know that all of us who have been baptized into Christ Jesus were baptized into his death? We were buried therefore with him by baptism into death, in order that, just as Christ was raised from the dead by the glory of the Father, we too might walk in

---

5. Luther, *Small Catechism*, 23.

newness of life" (Rom 6:3–4). That is, Holy Baptism is a true mark of the church through which God works to join the believer to Christ. God says that those who are baptized into Christ have "been buried with him in baptism, in which you were also raised with him through faith in the powerful working of God, who raised him from the dead" (Col 2:12).

This mark of the church, therefore, is a guarantee to the believer. It is one thing to hear the word of Christ and by the Spirit's power be given faith to hold to Christ, but it is another thing to experience the ensuing battle with the sinful nature and the confrontation with the world and the devil which causes undulation in the life of the believer. When such waves come, it is Holy Baptism which gives the believer the assurance that because they are sealed, they shall not fall. In effect, baptism is a living seal guaranteeing the believer that they are always joined to Christ no matter what happens to them in life.

The second mark of the church is therefore a poured-out word that seals the child of God to Christ with the promise that what God has done through baptism cannot be undone.

HOLY COMMUNION / THE LORD'S SUPPER

Holy Baptism was prescribed by God as being given once (Eph 4:5) as a sacrament of *initiation*, but even with God's seal upon them, believers are still susceptible to being shaken and upset by their sinful nature. God in his mercy therefore has provided Holy Communion (the Lord's Supper) as a sacrament of *continuation* to keep Christians sustained and strengthened along life's way. This mark of the church is the climactic aspect of every Sunday Divine Service.

Saint Ambrose said, "Because I always sin, I always need to take the medicine."[6] Whereas from God's panoramic perspective his children being forgiven means they are always forgiven, from our perspective in time, however, we need assurance that the forgiveness we have already received still stands in the present and into the future.

We are, of course, accustomed to this pattern. In returning to our marriage analogy, it will not do for a husband to be careless. If his wife asks, "Do you still love me?" he should not say, "Of course I do. I married you didn't I?" While this might true, it is probably not the answer his beloved is seeking. We are creatures who need present assurances of what has been

---

6. Augsburg Confession, Article 24. McCain et al., *Lutheran Confessions*, 49.

given in the past. It is as if we live with a constant anxiety towards change and potential change.

In the Lord's Supper, Christ is saying, "I am serious about my promise to never leave you nor forsake you! Here, I come to you again and again giving you my body and blood which I once gave on Calvary's cross. I give it to you regularly and frequently to keep you in the forgiveness of sins given to you when you were baptized into my name." His gift to us in the Lord's Supper is so important that the Holy Scriptures records Christ's institution of it *four* times (Matt 26:26–28, Mark 14:22–24, Luke 22:19–20, 1 Cor 11:23–25).

The third mark of the church is therefore an ongoing feast of God guaranteeing that his love and mercy for his people will never fade and through it keeps faith in God alive and strong.

THE OFFICE OF THE KEYS

The true church on earth demonstrates a fourth mark that is an office which exercises "keys," or God's authority to either release people from the bondage of sin or to keep them in it. This office is taught by Christ to the apostles:

- "I will give you the keys of the kingdom of heaven, and whatever you bind on earth shall be bound in heaven, and whatever you loose on earth shall be loosed in heaven" (Matt 16:19).
- "Truly, I say to you, whatever you bind on earth shall be bound in heaven, and whatever you loose on earth shall be loosed in heaven" (Matt 18:18).
- "And when he had said this, he breathed on them and said to them, 'Receive the Holy Spirit. If you forgive the sins of any, they are forgiven them; if you withhold forgiveness from any, it is withheld" (John 20:22–23).

Some people might think they have spotted an unnecessary redundancy: if Holy Communion is given for constant forgiveness throughout the undulations of life, isn't this office of the keys essentially doing the same thing?

First, one reason why the fourth mark of the church is unique is because there are times that a person is so plagued by doubt that they are best served through direct and personal absolution. But isn't the third mark of Holy Communion both direct and personal? It is, but what the fourth mark of the church gives is the opportunity for the child of God to come confessing deeply personal sins that represent a load so formidable that shame and guilt might otherwise keep these sins hidden and bound.

This mark is the living testimony that God never tires of keeping his people in the forgiveness of sins. Once, Saint Peter asked Christ if he should forgive an offending brother "as many as seven times" (Matt 18:21). Jesus answered Peter, "I do not say to you seven times, but seventy-seven times" (Matt 18:22). The Lord's answer was not for setting a new limit but to say that there is no limit to God's forgiveness.

Another reason why the office of the keys is not redundant in the face of Holy Communion is because of its other function—namely, the binding of sins. If one who confesses faith in Christ and membership in the church chooses to remain in sin—that is, the deliberate practice and lifestyle against the will and word of God—then that person is subject to churchly discipline through the office of the keys.

This says to all members of the church that God's people have been called to live in accord with the word of God. Saint Paul asks a rhetorical question: "What shall we say then? Are we to continue to sin that grace may abound? By no means!" (Rom 6:1–2a).

The fourth mark of the church is therefore an ongoing empirical practice which delivers God's inexhaustible love and mercy. It is also the real-world declaration that God's people are called to honor God with their lives. God says, "Those who honor me I will honor, and those who despise me shall be lightly esteemed" (1 Sam 2:30). This empirical mark therefore says to the world that God's people are comforted by constant forgiveness and are driven not to fall back into sin.

THE OFFICE OF THE MINISTRY

The fifth mark of the church is the office of the ministry. It is closely related to the fourth, but whereas the fourth mark is manifest by the office of Christ in action, the fifth mark of the church is marked by the office of Christ in the flesh. This mark of the church might be one of the hardest to recognize as the true work of the Holy Spirit in the church today.

It is not unusual for God's people to be in despair and distress. When their pain is palpable, they may ask, "Where is God?" But if they ask this question in the presence of their pastor, the answer is, "Right here with you!" God is present in his office, and he works through his called servants in fulfillment of his promise to never leave his people.

Again, this requires faith to see because in and of themselves, these fleshly manifestations of Christ's office are incredibly ordinary. They are mere men, *but the office they serve in is no mere office.* This is where the significance of this mark comes in: these mere men carry with them the holy ministry of God's church while preaching Christ's word and administering Christ's Sacraments. Through these means of grace, the Holy Spirit works powerfully to shower God's people with grace and the movement of God in their lives. All these gifts are managed through weak and frail servants, the fleshly who serve Christ's office.

This fifth mark of the church is therefore another real sign of the God who is there. Through these, God does not serve in a ghostly or ethereal way, but through the real voices, real hands, and real lives of servants fully perceived through whom all served by them may say with confidence, "The office of Christ is here with me because his called and ordained servant is here with me." This is because Jesus said to his first called servants, "The one who hears you hears me" (Luke 10:16).

CORPORATE WORSHIP

All the marks of the church give answer to the skeptics who ask, "Where is God?" These marks are all felt and experienced in real life: the real word goes into ears, Holy Baptism is a real seal that hits the forehead and guarantees union with Christ, Holy Communion is the real meal of the Savior who gives his real body and blood to keep his children in forgiveness, the office of the keys is the real absolution imputed upon the sinner for releasing them from the real burden of sin confessed, and the office of the ministry brings a real flesh-and-blood servant to serve God's child with God's real gifts of word and Sacrament. These gifts and manifestations of the love of God are as real as real can be. Where is God? Look! He is in these marks of his church.

The sixth mark, however, is an expression of every Christian being part and parcel of God's marks. The author of the book of Hebrews admonished Christians in the first century, "And let us consider how to stir up one another to love and good works, not neglecting to meet together, as is the habit of some, but encouraging one another, and all the more as you see the Day drawing near" (Heb 10:24–25).

When the children of God gather, they are fulfillments of God's promise never to leave his people. On the last day, Jesus will say, "Truly, I say to you, as you did it to one of the least of these my brothers, you did it to me" (Matt 25:40). That is, when God's people serve one another, it is another expression of Christ serving the other. If one sees someone else bringing them food, praying for or with them, or worshiping with them, then this is evidence that God is present in their life.

THE HOLY CROSS

The last mark of the church is the one every Christian carries out into the world. While we live in the estates or realms of the world which include the family, congregation, and state, the child of God is called to serve their neighbor whether that neighbor knows God or not. When the follower of Christ conducts this service, it will often come with a wide variety of difficulties and pressures. However, when the child of God carries out their callings faithfully despite hardships, they are also faithfully bearing a cross. That is, the child of God serves even when a big part of them doesn't want to. They endure the burden of crosses, their holy callings, in order to do the right thing and to live out the priority of serving their neighbor with the love of Christ even as the manifestation of this *agape*-love is uniquely expressed within the estates established by God.[7]

But to do this represents that followers of God do not follow the preoccupation with self which the world promotes. The world urges people to make life all about themselves. If anyone goes along with this way of thinking, they will, ironically, lose themselves in the most unhealthy and destructive way. The real "I"—the essential "I" (stage three)—is expressed in the new creation that comes when one is united to Jesus.

This new life, however, is yet another powerful and beautiful evidence that God is alive and well in the world. This is yet another mark of the church when the church ventures out into the world. And through this mark, people can see and perhaps come to know, "Yes, the God who is there is real. We can see him through his people."

The new life, however, is also a real life. A life with God's forgiveness permeating lives so that the new life overflows even through bodies. And God's holy people with their holy bodies will be raised again just as Christ was raised. To this part of the creed we now turn.

---

7. The subject matter of Espinosa, *Faith That Shines*.

CHAPTER 9 DISCUSSION GUIDE: CONTENDING FOR THE HOLY CHRISTIAN CHURCH

UNCOVER INFORMATION

1. What does the true church go through on earth?
2. Describe the church in Corinth.
3. What does the devil do in response to the true church?
4. What did Luther ask God *not* to send him?
5. How many marks of the church are there? Please list them.

DISCOVER MEANING

1. What is a "disciple"?
2. Why is it important that the marks of the church be identifiable and unmistakable?
3. What is the "one thing needful/necessary" which Jesus identified as recorded at Luke 10:41–42?
4. What does Holy Baptism join the Christian to?
5. If a Christian has a pastor, in what sense does that Christian always know where God is to be found?

EXPLORE IMPLICATIONS

1. Since Christ asked Saul, "Why are you persecuting me?" what does this say about Christ's relationship with his church?
2. What is implied about God's love for us that he gives the church so many marks?
3. What of a "church" in which the true word of Christ is not present?
4. If a Christian is by definition a person who has already received the forgiveness of sins, why does Christ commend all Christians to receive Holy Communion over and over again?

5. Choose any of the four remaining marks of the church. How does the mark you chose uniquely contribute to our endurance in the saving faith?

10

Contending for Our Same Bodies Raised

"I believe in God, . . . the Holy Spirit, . . . the forgiveness of sins,
the resurrection of the body . . ."

SHAPE-SHIFTING AGAINST THE GOSPEL OF CHRIST

In a past volume, I shared about the most gifted evangelist I've ever met in my friend and colleague, Rev. Mark Jasa. He employs a basic approach for sharing the gospel: get to what people can relate to universally in terms of the human experience. No one needs a college degree in religion to know that things like guilt, shame, and having to face death are real universal issues within anyone with a conscience. With these things identified, then share the gospel, the good news of Christ, and just ask these questions:

1. For whom did Christ die? Answer: all people.
2. For what sins did Christ pay for? Answer: all sins.
3. Which of your sins did Christ forget to pay for? Answer: none![1]

However, recall chapter 2 where we discussed the "shape-shifting" ways of the world. Recall the fictional "Borg" from *Star Trek* used as an illustration of how the word of Christ is countered in the culture. The Borg aliens were programmed and able to adapt to enemy attack and, furthermore, were

---

1. My discussion about Reverend Jasa and his basic approach in sharing the gospel is presented in Espinosa, *Faith That Engages.*

experts at regeneration while adapting. The bottom line is that they adjusted so that they found a way to keep coming at whomever was resisting.

Even Satan shape-shifted against Christ, eventually adjusting his temptation towards Christ by quoting his own word against him! This is the audacity that characterizes shape-shifting. It will take any means necessary to reject the gospel even while maintaining a deeply religious and spiritual veneer.

This is exactly what happens within our culture today. It is, therefore, not surprising that the basic approach to sharing the saving gospel of Jesus Christ has been countered by a significant shape-shift in our culture today.

ENTER REINCARNATION

The transmigration of the soul at physical death from one body to another (reincarnation) has been attached to both Hinduism and Buddhism for millennia. At the same time, it is a worldview that has only grown in Western culture and furthermore is an aggressive shape-shifter towards the word of Christ.

In response to the universally shared experiences of guilt and shame, there is once again the bona fide response of natural religion: these must be worked out in consideration of one's *karma* (acts, works, and deeds).[2] There is, however, an enormous caveat: one can experience many lifetimes or rebirths to cleanse oneself to be able to achieve oneness with Brahman or the overarching experience of being one with God. Sometimes reincarnation is dressed up as a version of Christianity so that a person can become "Christ" (as Jesus *became* "Christ"), as put forth by Elizabeth Clare Prophet.[3] All this, of course, is contrary to the word of God.

What is perhaps the even more dangerous caveat is that the fear of death is deceptively quelled. At first blush, the understanding that human beings are more than their bodies may seem liberating. And, by the way, to this, orthodox Christianity is in full agreement. The danger, however, comes in the teaching of reincarnation regarding the physical body. It is strictly temporary and transitory. That is, just as one might have a good coat or jacket but, in time, have it wear out, no problem. Though someone might have become attached to their old favorite coat or jacket, no one will mourn its loss when it comes time to buy a new one. The body in reincarnation is

---

2. See chapter 6 above on the major world religions summarized.
3. Prophet, *Reincarnation*, 46.

like a coat while in the Christian faith, the body is the temple of God that will be raised from death.

On this account, we can go back to Reverend Jasa's basic presentation of the gospel of Jesus Christ in the hearing of the reincarnationist. "Sin" is waylaid in that surely—given enough time and transmigrations of the soul—karma can be controlled. As for the fear of death, why fear it? If the essential self, which is spirit, continues beyond the body, there is nothing to fear. And this is exactly the progression that is so spectacularly dangerous.

THE IMPACT OF THE ATONEMENT OF CHRIST

When God finished creation, he looked upon all of it—and allow us to underline *all of it*—and called it good. As the Holy Scriptures record, "And God saw everything that he had made, and behold, it was very good. And there was evening and there was morning, the sixth day" (Gen 1:31). In that instance, physicality was deemed very good.

The Christian faith is not allergic toward the human body. It does not subjugate the material world to the spiritual arena as was the way of the Greeks. Because of this historical trend towards the presumption that the spiritual realm is superior to the physical, the incarnation of God in Christ was profoundly resisted.

The trend against Christ has been long. Arius argued that Jesus himself, the *Logos*, though preeminent in all creation was nevertheless created. This was an egregious heresy denying the eternal progression of the Son from the Father and rejecting that Jesus is by nature very God of very God. Jesus was not created. How could he be created since he is the Creator (Col 1:15–16)?

Greek diminution of the body was also seen in the heresy known as Docetism from the Greek *dokeo* which means "to seem," as in "have the appearance."[4] This teaching was that Jesus only seemed or appeared to have a physical body. In this view, how could God have a body since from a Greek perspective, the body is not worthy of the nature of divinity?

When others who wanted to abide more closely to the biblical teaching on the person of Christ realized that the Bible would not compromise Jesus' real human body, the heretic Cerinthus came along to qualify Docetism: Jesus indeed had a human body, but the divine spirit that entered him at his baptism also departed from him at his crucifixion. Thus, any talk of

---

4. BAGD 202.

Christ's "divinity" is limited to a divine spirit. What this heresy could never say is that the person, Jesus Christ, was always God in the flesh.

Gnosticism is bedfellows with the several attempts to compromise Christ's humanity because the goal of "Christ" was not atonement, but rather the imparting of secret knowledge. And what was this secret knowledge (*gnosis*) for? It was for the application of that knowledge to guide the spirit in such a way as to release it from the limitations of the body, again presuming the inferiority of the body.

But in addition to the fact that God declared his entire creation "very good," the atonement of Christ was a salvific work done for the complete restoration of the entire very good creation. Christ atoned for humanity's sin—covered it with his blood—and became one with humanity so that the physical body would be what God originally intended it to be: eternal, just like the spirit.

In other words, the Christian faith defines a person as someone intended for eternal life with a body and spirit designed to live eternally. To separate these is to rip apart what it means to be human. A person is a person because they are body *and* spirit.

To compromise the body is also to profane the atonement of Jesus Christ. The forgiveness of sins is not simply a cancellation of debt towards God for violating his will and love for us, but it is also the restoration and healing of our body and spirit. There is nothing that demonstrates the resultant healing and restoration better than the resurrection of the Lord Jesus Christ himself.

CHRIST'S RESURRECTION COUNTERS REINCARNATION

Of course, in chapter 7 we looked at the historical foundations for the resurrection of Christ, but here we are applying its application to the resurrection of everyone else.[5] To be precise about this application, it must be said that Christ's bodily resurrection eliminates the possibility of reincarnation.

The Christ who rose was the exact same Savior as the Christ who was crucified. This was a superlative foregone conclusion. Saint Thomas intrinsically knew that for Jesus Christ to be Jesus Christ, then the one who was crucified had to be the same one who rose. This famously cited example

---

5. Everyone will rise. Some will rise with the unjust and others will rise with the just. Some will rise while continuing to reject the grace of God, while others will rise continuing to hold to the grace of God.

of apostolic doubt could be seen to double up as the most invaluable testimony to the sameness of persons who die and rise. This is something we must thank God for and perhaps also Saint Thomas:

> Now Thomas, one of the twelve, called the Twin, was not with them when Jesus came. So the other disciples told him, "We have seen the Lord." But he said to them, "Unless I see in his hands the mark of the nails, and place my finger into the mark of the nails, and place my hand into his side, I will never believe." Eight days later, his disciples were inside again, and Thomas was with them. Although the doors were locked, Jesus came and stood among them and said, "Peace be with you." Then he said to Thomas, "Put your finger here, and see my hands; and put out your hand, and place it in my side. Do not disbelieve, but believe." Thomas answered him, "My Lord and my God!" (John 20:24–28)

How would Saint Thomas verify that this was Jesus Christ? It would come upon the examination of Christ's *body*. He knew that there could be no speaking of resurrection without the same body of the same person having returned from death.

This demonstration of the law of noncontradiction between the incompatibility of resurrection and reincarnation is also highlighted by the fact that God in his caring providence permitted some people during the earthly ministry of Jesus to die and be raised back to life in their bodies. In every single case, there was no question as to the identity of who was raised: it was always the same person—with the same body—who died.

That is, we know this to be the case in considering the law of noncontradiction:

Either: Joe dies and is raised as Joe.

Or: Joe dies and is reincarnated as someone else.

It does no good to try to find a default through the "spirit of Joe" being maintained because reincarnation has now deserted the "in the same sense and at the same time" of the law of noncontradiction. That is, the definition of "person" is completely altered, not only because new bodies may be introduced to a person but also because ultimately no body is needed at all in becoming a part of "god" as the consummate goal in reincarnation.[6]

---

6. Of course, "part of God" descriptors are in and of themselves problematic. In reincarnation, "God" himself is evolving as people have the potential to become a part of "him." "We are *unformed* Gods and Goddesses. And we all have the opportunity to enter,

PART III | THIRD ARTICLE OF THE CREED

WHAT ABOUT ELIJAH?

Perhaps the most celebrated argument—in reference to the Holy Bible—used by reincarnationists is the account of John the Baptist and Elijah. Christ taught,

> Truly, I say to you, among those born of women there has arisen no one greater than John the Baptist. Yet the one who is least in the kingdom of heaven is greater than he. From the days of John the Baptist until now the kingdom of heaven has suffered violence, and the violent take it by force. For all the Prophets and the Law prophesied until John, and if you are willing to accept it, he is Elijah who is to come. (Matt 11:11–14)

In this section of God's word, the Lord Jesus reinforced the prophecy of Micah: "Behold, I will send you Elijah the prophet before the great and awesome day of the Lord comes" (Mic 4:5). Reincarnation purports that in these teachings, John the Baptist was Elijah reincarnated.

Elijah, the great prophet of the Old Testament who was carried to God on a chariot of fire (2 Kgs 2:11–12), is the one referred to both by Christ and by Micah. Of course, the question that must be asked is, "In what *sense* does Elijah come again?" Hermeneutical principles guide the interpretative process. For example, *scriptura scripturam interpretatur* ("Scripture interprets Scripture") demands that other Scriptural passages related to our consideration be consulted.

For example, the idea of Elijah being reincarnated in John seems quite unlikely by another related passage. At the onset of the Baptist's ministry, priests and Levites from Jerusalem confronted him asking point blank, "Are you Elijah?" to which John replied, "I am not" (John 1:21).

So how is one person another without being the same person? The answer is far less complicated than reincarnation. An angel of the Lord had informed Zechariah the priest that he and his wife, Elizabeth, would have a son named John (Luke 1:13), and that his son "will go before [the Lord] in the spirit and power of Elijah" (Luke 1:17). This descriptor of "spirit and power" means that John the Baptist in *his* ministry will be in alignment with and like that of Elijah in *his* ministry.

---

portion by portion, into a mystical union with that divine spark. If we look at our lives as a process of reconstructing our God Self, then we can claim to be Gods in the making rather than Gods in ruin." Prophet, *Reincarnation*, 40.

This is not unlike the situation recorded in Deut 18. Moses was one of the greatest prophets who ever lived. With him, the Lord God spoke face-to-face (Exod 33:11), and he was also a prophet through whom God worked mighty miracles. Obviously, as a prophet, Moses also spoke God's word to God's people.

On one occasion, God said through Moses, as Moses prophesied to Israel, "The Lord your God will raise up for you a prophet like me from among you, from your brothers—it is to him you shall listen" (Deut 18:15). Jesus also came as Moses in the sense that he too was (1) sent from God, (2) raised up from the Hebrews, and (3) would speak the word of God. He was like Moses but greater than Moses. Their ministries, however, had many common intersections. The same was true between Elijah and John the Baptist.

Furthermore, in Mark's gospel Christ's words that treat John the Baptist and Elijah side by side come immediately after the event of the transfiguration. At the transfiguration, Peter, James, and John see Moses and Elijah standing alongside Christ in radiant light. Their appearance is not random. One way the entire Old Testament was referred to was by the designation "the Law and the Prophets." Moses represents the Law/Pentateuch/Torah and Elijah represents the Prophets. Both the Law and Prophets of the Old Testament had pointed to Jesus, and these two leaders were giving testimony again to the Christ, the Savior of the world, on the Mount of Transfiguration.

That is, Elijah was still fully Elijah in glory. Moses was still Moses. And we can rest assured that John the Baptist was still John the Baptist. The significance regarding reincarnation is that Elijah had gone to heavenly glory long before John the Baptist was born. Moreover, John the Baptist had died before Elijah appeared at the transfiguration. That is, Elijah remained Elijah, and his personal identity suffered no fluctuation. He remained consistently himself, not only regarding his spirit but also his body, even through his assumption into glory on the chariots of fire (2 Kgs 2:11).

The echo of everything we've discussed here about one going forth as another has not changed. It is a major mode of operation of God for his church. When pastors in the true church administer the sacraments of the church, they speak in the first person:

1. For Holy Absolution: "I forgive you all your sins..."
2. For Holy Baptism: "I baptize you in the Name..."
3. For Holy Communion: "This is my body, this is my blood..."

The called and ordained pastors speak for Jesus himself. Their word in these instances are Jesus' words; the authority they transmit is the authority of God; the office they act in is Christ's office. They are—in these instances, one could say—Jesus. And yet, and at the same time, they are in no way Jesus ontologically. They are most certainly not Jesus reincarnated.

THE OFFENSIVE JESUS

Who Jesus truly is and what Jesus truly did is offensive to human reason. God's categories don't fit into ours. And this is the way God wants it. This way, we should never think God must submit to human reason.[7] If he did, then it would only be a matter of time before we considered ourselves divine, which is exactly the trajectory of reincarnation.

Saint Paul wrote in respect to the work of Christ on the cross, "For the word of the cross is folly to those who are perishing, but to us who are being saved it is the power of God" (1 Cor 1:18).

God isn't being cruel in taking this approach; rather, he is exerting his justice in the face of rebellion. "For since, in the wisdom of God, the world did not know God through wisdom, it pleased God through the folly of what we preach to save those who believe" (1 Cor 1:21). Against such rebellion, Saint Paul affirmed the necessity of the "offense of the cross" for those who insist that their works merit salvation (Gal 5:11).

The perspective of reincarnation fits the bill of what Paul was warning against. The Christ of Holy Scripture is folly to reincarnationists because he doesn't fit into their multi-rebirth schema. As a result, and within this view, the person of Christ—who he actually *is*—is patently denied.

Elizabeth Clare Prophet teaches, "The reincarnationists saw Jesus as a man who showed us how to become one with God."[8] In the meantime, the reincarnationist believes that they may also be Christ: "I see all of us as sons of God who have the potential to become the Christ as Jesus did. Christhood is not something unique to Jesus. . . . We, too, can become one with the Logos, in other words, become the Christ, and be called Sons of God."[9]

---

7. This is not to say that Christianity is not coherent, logical, nor reasonable. If miracles are possible, then everything Christianity teaches is consistent within its doctrine as a whole.

8. Prophet, *Reincarnation*, 46.

9. Prophet, *Reincarnation*, 46.

As much as the transmigration of the soul position refers to "Christ," Jesus is denied as THE Christ. In turn, the Johannine warning applies here: "Who is the liar but he who denies that Jesus is the Christ? This is the antichrist, he who denies the Father and the Son" (1 John 2:2).

Of course, the split second the person of Christ is rejected, his work is likewise denied. No mere man could atone for the sins of the world. Reincarnationists rather—in holding to natural religion—must maintain human responsibility for addressing one's karma.

Erin Prophet, the daughter of Elizabeth Clare Prophet, wrote the foreword for her mother's volume previously cited. There, she expresses incredulity toward the real Christ. She asks two questions in particular:

> And if Jesus can simply wipe away all of our past mistakes, is there a point to our actions on earth? . . . If we really have only one shot at eternity in either heaven or hell, what happens to those of us whose lives are cut short by war or cancer?[10]

Unfortunately, these are precisely the sorts of false dilemmas which arise while pushing back the real Savior. The atonement of Christ does nothing to cancel the value of our lives and actions. In fact, the atonement renders our lives invaluable, the object of the greatest love the world has ever known in the Father sending his Son for them.

At the same time, the actions of those who are in Christ similarly take on eternal significance. Not only were the good works of God's people prepared by God in advance for them to do (Eph 2:10), but those same works follow after them into heaven (Rev 14:13). As for the works of those rebelling against God, the personal responsibility for those who do them remains completely intact. The point here is evidence that God's judgement is just.

Of course, this segues into Erin's second question above which is also complemented by another question her mother, Elizabeth, asks, "For Christianity has had difficulty answering the question 'What happens to someone who dies neither good enough for heaven nor bad enough for hell?'"[11]

The questions relate to both quantity (time) and quality (actions, good or evil) in respect to life, and both miss how both aspects are addressed in God's holy word. The idea of a life cut short is real from our perspective, but not God's. Again, for God, a day is as a thousand years and a thousand years

---

10. Prophet, *Reincarnation*, xvii.
11. Prophet, *Reincarnation*, 15.

as a day (2 Pet 3:8). Even a child's life, which from our vantage point may be cut tragically short, is nevertheless of inestimable value to God.

The Christian church, of course, must always stand up for those who cannot speak for themselves (Prov 31:8). Disciples of Jesus cannot condone abortion on demand. In fact, one of the manifest tragedies of reincarnation is the inherent sanitation of abortion. After all, why is the aborted child a tragedy if they will simply experience the transmigration of their soul? Such logic will not stand before God in judgment.

In the meantime, the Christian church must guard against Erin Prophet's "one shot" at heaven complaint. Here, we need to take stock of the facts. It is estimated that the average adult has somewhere between six thousand to seventy thousand thoughts per day, and it is not uncommon to have more than one thought at the same time. This means that if an adult lived for seventy years (while having the minimum one thought at a time), they would have somewhere in the range of 153,000,000 to 1,789,000,000 thoughts in their lifetime.

Now, consider this: *one* thought coupled to a living faith which confesses, "I trust you Lord Jesus with my forgiveness and eternal life" would be enough to indicate someone's life as crossing over from death to life in Christ. In this view, how many "one shots" does one need?

As for that hypothetical person "who dies neither good enough for heaven nor bad enough for hell," we enter an outright category mistake. It is like asking, "What does square taste like?" As a university professor I have said aloud many times to insecure students too timid to ask questions, "There is no such thing as a bad question." I confess here and now that I have exaggerated in those instances. There are!

Elizabeth Clare Prophet's question is in this category for a couple reasons:

1. *No one* except for Christ is good enough for heaven.

2. *Everyone* save Christ is bad enough for hell.

Once again, the *reason* her questions sound reasonable is on account of the presumption of righteousness or the condition of natural religion. But heaven cannot be merited since it requires perfection. Therefore, no one may enter heaven apart from the atonement of Christ, which identifies those who hold to Christ through faith as one with him and are therefore, marked by *his* perfection *for* them.

As for hell, our sinful nature delights in the comparison that some are worse than others. But God will not play that game. There were among the religious elite in the days of Jesus those who thought they were righteous on account of their outward appearances. They were quite certain in themselves that they were not anywhere as sinful as prostitutes and tax collectors. Jesus would not permit their delusion. He told them, "The tax collectors and the prostitutes go into the kingdom of God before you" (Matt 21:31).

They were enmeshed in their own pride to the extent that they could not see their true condition. Christ gave them this diagnosis in love that they might repent, "So you also outwardly appear righteous to others but within you are full of hypocrisy and lawlessness" (Matt 23:28).

The moment we realize that we are unworthy of heaven and worthy of hell, we may be permitted by the Holy Spirit to despair of ourselves. Then, as we give up on the presumption of righteousness and natural religion, we may call on the Lord Jesus Christ. In that instance we may trust that what he has already accomplished for all people—atoning for all sins of all people—is also credited to anyone who takes hold of this truth for themselves. At the end of the day, the God who is there is the God of grace offering this:

> Complete forgiveness of all sins on account of his Son, Jesus, through faith in him alone apart from all *karma* or other works.

Instead of this:

> The need to work out one's *karma* for rebirth after rebirth after rebirth.

The former approach reflects love and mercy, the latter approach reflects probation and withholding of release.

BUT WHAT ABOUT?

There is still one thing in particular causing the reincarnationist to resist the God who is there: the reported phenomena of remembering past lives. We revisit a Scripture mentioned before:

> The coming of the lawless one is by the activity of Satan with all power and false signs and wonders, and with all wicked deception for those who are perishing, because they refused to love the truth and so be saved. Therefore God sends them a strong delusion, so

that they may believe what is false, in order that all may be condemned who did not believe the truth but had pleasure in unrighteousness. (2 Thess 2:9–12)

It is important to note that God does not deny experiential phenomena, nor does he qualify that it would not be powerful nor convincing, but these are entirely beside the point.

The God who is there has provided revelation for us elsewhere that trains us about what we might experience as human beings on planet earth:

> When you come into the land that the Lord your God is giving you, you shall not learn to follow the abominable practices of those nations. There shall not be found among you anyone who burns his son or his daughter as an offering, anyone who practices divination or tells fortunes or interprets omens, or a sorcerer or a charmer or a medium or a necromancer or one who inquires of the dead, for whoever does these things is an abomination to the Lord. And because of these abominations the Lord your God is driving them out before you. (Deut 18:9–12)

Nowhere in this pericope does God say that these practices do not emit some kind of real power. Neither does God deny that those who gravitate towards these practices will not experience real phenomena. God did not prohibit these things because they were not powerful, but because they were and could produce in themselves a life-destroying delusion. Should we be surprised? Saint Paul warns, "And no wonder, for even Satan disguises himself as an angel of light" (2 Cor 11:14).

Once when Moses and Aaron stood before Pharaoh King of Egypt, they laid down God's staff to demonstrate to Pharaoh the power of God. But Pharaoh countered it: "Then Pharaoh summoned the wise men and sorcerers, and they, the magicians of Egypt, also did the same by their secret arts" (Exod 7:11). The God who is there, however, would not permit Pharaoh's power play to go unanswered: "But Aaron's staff swallowed up their staffs" (Exod 7:12). And much more importantly, God's ten plagues eventually surpassed the ability of the practitioners of the dark arts to replicate his work and in each case showed his superiority over the gods of Egypt (Exod 7–12).

In the meantime, it must be understood that the existence of exceptional phenomena by no means guarantees a benign source behind the phenomena. Other phenomena also occur. For example, near-death experiences can be interpreted in a variety of ways and can easily mislead.

At physical death, there is indeed separation, *but on the last day, there is a reunion of the same spirit with the same body so that the same person who is in Christ is raised in glory at the resurrection.* We know this on account of the real Christ. Saint Paul testifies, "But in fact Christ has been raised from the dead, the firstfruits of those who have fallen asleep" (1 Cor 15:20).

That is, what happened to Jesus will happen for those who belong to him: they shall die as whomever they are in accord with their personal identities in a particular body. They (like Jesus) shall be raised again as the same person with the same body now glorified.[12] Again, because Jesus set the pace as the "firstfruits," his children will follow in his train.

This truth, however, does not mean that those apart from Christ will not also rise. They will, too, but in such a way that they will experience the calamity of the conventional wisdom, "Be careful what you wish for." That is, God who is both just and merciful will grant what is preferred over real life in Christ. What is granted, however, ought not be construed as a good thing.

In the meantime, wisdom reigns: "There is a way that seems right to a man, but its end is the way to death" (Prov 14:12). The God who is there is merciful and proclaims, "Today, if you hear his voice, do not harden your hearts" (Heb 4:7).

CHAPTER 10 DISCUSSION GUIDE: CONTENDING FOR OUR SAME BODIES RAISED

UNCOVER INFORMATION

1. How did the devil "shape-shift" while confronting Jesus in the wilderness?
2. What is the belief called "reincarnation?"
3. What did the ancient Greeks believe about the body in comparison to the spirit?
4. When God declared the creation very good, was the human body included in God's declaration?
5. Who is good enough for heaven? Who is bad enough for hell?

---

12. But what of bodies deformed or in some way subject to horrible disease and plagues? We shall consider this in the upcoming chapter.

DISCOVER MEANING

1. In what sense was John the Baptist Elijah?
2. By insisting on reincarnation, what kind of religion is being held onto? This is also called by Luther "the presumption of _____?"
3. Why was the teaching of _____ (name the heretic) about Christ heretical?
4. How might the reality of God permitting most people millions and millions of thoughts reflect his mercy?
5. How might the Christian classify the memory of past lives?

EXPLORE IMPLICATIONS

1. If reincarnation were true, what of the divinity of Christ / the real Christ?
2. By comparing our body to a coat or jacket, what is reincarnation implying about the human body?
3. Why are resurrection and reincarnation incompatible?
4. How might the Christian answer the objection that the Christian faith gives people only "one shot" at heaven?
5. How does reincarnation reinforce abortion on demand?

11

Contending for the Life Everlasting

"I believe in God, the Father, . . . Jesus Christ, . . . the Holy Spirit, . . .
and the life everlasting."

THE OFFENSE OF HEAVEN

If God is despised, his gifts will be despised, and if God is mocked, what he has prepared for his people will be mocked. Because God is blasphemed, heaven is an object of the world's scorn and pessimism. Because Jesus said to his children, "Rejoice and be glad, for your reward is great in heaven" (Matt 5:12a), heaven—and not a mere immortality of the soul and that which is the opposite of the reality of hell—must be scorned as much as God in the flesh.

The Lord Jesus once encountered such attitudes from a Jewish sect that denied the resurrection of the body and the place of heaven:

> The same day Sadducees came to him, who say that there is no resurrection, and they asked him a question, saying, "Teacher, Moses said, 'If a man dies having no children, his brother must marry the widow and raise up offspring for his brother.' Now there were seven brothers among us. The first married and died, and having no offspring left his wife to his brother. So too the second and third, down to the seventh. After them all, the woman died. In the resurrection, therefore, of the seven, whose wife will she be? For they all had her." But Jesus answered them, "You are wrong, because you know neither the Scriptures nor the power of God.

Part III | Third Article of the Creed

For in the resurrection they neither marry nor are given in marriage, but are like the angels in heaven." (Matt 22:23–30)

The Sadducees thought the implications of heaven were ludicrous. Jesus reveals why they did: they knew neither the Scriptures nor the power of God. The Holy Scriptures declare, however, "what no eye has seen, nor ear heard, nor the heart of man imagined, what God has prepared for those who love him" (1 Cor 2:9).

But when a person does *not* love the God who is there, then anything coming from his word will be remain suspect. And what is suspect is easily ridiculed. As a result, heaven is criticized:

1. As a place without essential humanity or free will
2. As a place without beauty or wonderful expression
3. As a place without exhilaration, but full of tedium

All these concerns can be addressed at the same time. Since God created us, he might know a thing or two about preparing a place for us where we would *want* to be. In fact, when we take the words of the psalmist into consideration, "You make known to me the path of life; in your presence there is fullness of joy; at your right hand are pleasures forevermore" (Ps 16:11), then heaven is the place we yearn to be.

When Jesus comforted the thief on the cross right before they both died, he said, "Truly, I say to you, today you will be with me in paradise" (Luke 23:43). Heaven is *the* real paradise.

It is also the place in which our full humanity will not only stay intact but will know a wholeness and perfection never before attained;[1] it has a beauty and radiance so wonderful that what is heard from this place is too great to be told on earth (2 Cor 12:4); and it is the last place boredom could ever exist. It will bring the constancy of the fullness of joy, that plane of experience in which we never want to leave.

Unlike Saint Paul, who evidently received a glimpse of heavenly glory (2 Cor 12:2),[2] I nevertheless received an object lesson that is easily applied to our discussion about heaven from one of my daughters.

---

1. For example, Saint Paul lists the comparison between our bodies that die and our bodies that will be raised, leading to fully knowing Christ's victory over death and sin in 1 Cor 15:42–58.

2. The expression "third heaven" mentioned in 2 Cor 12:2 does not suggest degrees or levels of heaven, but the paradise of which Christ spoke of and surpasses what is merely the invisible realm (think of the "heavenly places" in the spiritual battle described in Eph

When our fourth child, Christina, was only about three years old, we were blessed to have an annual family pass to Disneyland. The timing was perfect for my little "Bean," as I affectionately call her. On my day off we would often make the most of the pass and take her to Disneyland. I feel as though I took her (holding her hand as we walked or carried her) over every square inch of the Magic Kingdom.

There's a media slogan referring to Disneyland as "The Happiest Place on Earth." I personally learned how untrue that slogan is because I realized there were only so many times I could hear the "It's a Small World" song without considering how I could jump off the boat and bolt for the exit.

But as dusk settled and my wife and I felt our legs getting heavy, I would turn to my Bean and ask her, "Are you ready to go home now?" This scene and question was repeated over and over again.

People will often say, "every single time," and most every time we realize we are listening to an exaggeration, but in this instance, I am not exaggerating. *Every single time* my little Bean answered me by saying, "No." Even if she was starting to get sleepy, she would say "No." She *never* wanted to leave.

My little analogy covers a few bases here:

1. My Bean was never kept at Disneyland against her will.
2. My Bean found the lights, colors, and beauty fantastic.
3. My Bean was excited during our visits and never bored.

And while "It's a Small World" may have scarred me for life, I was happy that my BEAN found so much joy in that place. That year was worth every minute of our time together in her special place before we moved away to another state the following year. My little girl gave me just a little glimpse of what our attitude might be like in a place that is infinitely more amazing than the place she never tired of on earth that year.

6:12); nor does it refer to the cosmos (the starry skies, the universe, etc.). It is instead the highest or best of all other places where God's people will be in the direct presence of God and his glory.

Part III | Third Article of the Creed

WHY WE REALLY COMPLAIN AND OUR CHERISHED "FREE WILL"

Sometimes our complaints about something are smoke screens for deeper issues. The problem with the presumption of righteousness is that it makes us want more control over what happens to us. We want to pave our own path and carve out our own lives. We want to plan our own vacations. We want to determine our own destinies.

For this to happen, nothing becomes more sacred in the realm of man-made religion and faith than the idea of "free will." Interestingly, however, those two words—side by side—do not occur anywhere in Holy Scripture.

There is, of course, a kind of formal or worldly freedom known in the civil realm. We rise in the morning and choose to put on a blue outfit over a black one, we choose one political platform over another, or—with great wisdom and insight—choose to root for the Lakers over the Celtics. All these examples, however, are functional for our interaction with the world.

But this civil realm formal freedom does not transfer to our material or essential ability for "choosing" or "freely willing" to come to God. We might want it to, but that would be wishful thinking. Jesus said to his first disciples, "You did not choose me, but I chose you" (John 15:16). Prior to that in chapter 6, Jesus explained to his disciples that they came to him not by their own power but by the Father *giving* them to Christ (6:37, 39), the Father *drawing* them to Christ (v. 44), and that "no one can come to me unless it is granted him by the Father" (v. 65).

Why must this be the case? Because the human will is dominated by the sinful nature before conversion (stage two above) and will not by its own power—under any circumstances—be willing to come to God. In fact, it just can't. Before conversion, material or essential will in relation to God is in bondage. Luther wrote, "If we are under the god of this world, away from the work and Spirit of the true God, we are held captive to his will, as Paul says to Timothy [2 Tim 2:26], so that we cannot will anything but what he wills"[3] Conversely, in Christ we may have what Luther referred to as "royal freedom" to do readily what God wills.[4]

Saint Augustine put it another way that is in complete concert with the Scriptures and Luther, for that matter: "There is, however, always within us a free will, but it is not always good; for it is either free from righteousness

---

3. Luther, *Career of the Reformer*, 65.
4. Luther, *Career of the Reformer*, 65.

when it serves sin, and then it is evil, or else it is free from sin when it serves righteousness, and then it is good."[5]

This was Saint Augustine's way of correcting our ideas about "free will." That is, the condition of the human heart determines what is "free" about the human will. If the condition of the person is good, then they will know a will that freely serves good, but if the condition of the person is against God, then they will know a will that freely serves what is contrary to God.

But to insist that one may choose which condition they may be in is the epitome of the presumption of righteousness. The belief that we can make ourselves good is the belief of natural religion in all its glory. It does not need God because it can make itself good. Indeed, this thinking is at the root of all religions promoting human evolution towards divinity, confusing the creation with its Creator.

Heaven, however, is an eternal place where God in grace has permitted a person to have a transformed will that is one with God's will. Is freedom in this? Absolutely, because the person in heaven will freely live according to the grace of God for eternity. And already on this side of heaven, the people of the Living God begin to taste this freedom. They are not coerced to follow Christ, but they want to.

Thus, to the people of God according to their new lives in the Spirit, God's commandments are not burdensome (1 John 5:3). For the child of God, heaven is not a burden. It is not a prison nor a place where anything is forced.

It is also a place that has already been purchased for everyone because the real Savior shed his blood to purchase life and heaven for humanity. To simply trust in him is to know heaven as one's home, the place the people of God long for.

HEAVEN: A REAL COUNTRY AND CITY

God's word presents heaven as both a country and a city: "But as it is, they desire a better country, that is, a heavenly one. Therefore God is not ashamed to be called their God, for he has prepared for them a city" (Heb 11:16). In addition, Saint John, while employing the symbolism of Revelation, also describes heaven as a real city.

---

5. Augustine, *Grace and Free Will* 31 (NPNF[1] 5:456).

Part III | Third Article of the Creed

God teaches through the apostle that heaven at Christ's second advent will be a new heaven combined with a new earth (Rev 21:1). It is described as follows in the apocalypse:

1. It is a dwelling place for God and people together (Rev 21:3).
2. It is place where all sorrow, mourning, and death are gone (Rev 21:4), and nothing unclean will be there (Rev 21:27).
3. It will have the glory of God filling it and it will be a radiant place (Rev 21:11).
4. It has walls, foundations, and gates (Rev 21:12–15).
5. It is a city of pure gold like clear glass (Rev 21:18).
6. It has a street of pure gold like transparent glass (Rev 21:21).
7. It is filled with the light of God (Rev 21:23).
8. It will have the nations represented with their glory and honor (Rev 21:26).
9. It has the river of the water of life (Rev 22:1).
10. It has the tree of life, fruit, and healing leaves (Rev 22:2).

In the vision we learn that there is a kind of resemblance and correspondence between earthly things and heavenly things. Not only is this consistent with the original "very good" creation before sin entered creation (Gen 1:31), but it is even more significantly consistent with the resurrection of the Lord Jesus Christ.

His body that died was the same body raised, but it was raised in glory as opposed to a tattered or wounded state. This, too, gives indication that the new eternal heaven will have the most beautiful things of the first creation but be infinitely greater in splendor and magnificence. In the new eternal heaven, our bodies will be our bodies but in a form that is beyond what we can imagine. Saint Paul provides this description of our bodies from earth to heaven:

> What is sown is perishable; what is raised is imperishable. It is sown in dishonor; it is raised in glory. It is sown in weakness; it is raised in power. It is sown a natural body; it is raised a spiritual body. . . . This mortal body must put on immortality. (1 Cor 15:42–44, 53b)

Saint John states what is an even greater vision: "Beloved, we are God's children now, and what we will be has not yet appeared; but we know that when he appears we shall be like him, because we shall see him as he is" (1 John 3:2). While the distinction between Creator and his created people is eternally maintained, we will at the same time reflect the very glory of Christ in our bodies.

This holds fantastic ramifications. Bodies in this world and life that were subject to disease, deformity, and terrible injury will experience a restoration that simply wipes out what is perishable, dishonorable, weak, natural, and mortal. Wrecked bodies will become glorious bodies.

In addition, in glory, God's people will be completely recognizable in their bodies. This is almost an overwhelming mystery and yet it is in accord with God's true word. When Christ appeared in radiant light to Peter, James, and John at the transfiguration, the apostles were able to *recognize* Moses and Elijah. The issue here is that they were centuries removed from each other and had never previously met.

The restoration of our bodies into glorious bodies coincides with the restoration of our minds as glorious minds. The word of God teaches, "For now we see in a mirror dimly, but then face to face. Now I know in part; then I shall know fully, even as I have been fully known" (1 Cor 13:12).

We shall see others in Christ, including our loved ones who died in the Lord, in glorious bodies that we have never seen before, and yet we will have no trouble whatsoever recognizing them. Invariably, questions come about the babies or the very elderly and here the same answer is given: they too will have glorious bodies, and they too will be 100 percent recognizable.

This repulses sinful reason: "How dare God play with time this way!" But time is for God to do with as he pleases. If any of us had been able to bump into Adam on the day he was created, we would have met a fully mature man at the ripe old age of one day.

Heaven is also a place of fellowship, unity, and love. The Holy Scripture on the Sadducees confronting Christ includes the bit about how children of God will be like the angels (having no need to reproduce anymore) and therefore will neither marry nor be given in marriage. As great a vocation marriage was on earth—a vocation symbolizing the very relationship between Christ and his bride, the church—it is also a vocation that will be surpassed in heaven.

But what about intimacy? What about the various expressions of love which in themselves bring so much joy to people? What we know is this:

heaven is described as a "marriage" (Matt 25:10, Rev 19:9) and "a feast" (Isa 25:6, Matt 8:11, Luke 13:29), which is to say that there will be a fellowship, communion, and a sharing of love that is beyond our ability to describe. And this union with God and others will be so great it will surpass the surpassing joy inexpressible that the people of God already know in Christ (1 Pet 1:8). What will it be like exactly? We must wait, but it will be worth the wait.

Finally, will we know each other according to the stations we held on earth? Why not? If Peter, James, and John knew Moses and Elijah, they were surely also aware of their stations in the world, mighty prophets of God who led and defended Israel. So, why wouldn't we know our good and holy stations in life? Thus, while we may very well recognize a parent, a sibling, a spouse, a child in accord with their stations while we were on earth, there will be nothing—but *nothing*—to detract from or dim our perfect joy in heaven. Even while on earth, God's people knew that "love covers a multitude of sins" (1 Pet 4:8). How much more will this be the case in perfection?

THE OFFENSE OF HELL

God is not sadistic. God says, "Have I any pleasure in the death of the wicked . . . and not rather that he should turn from his way and live?" (Ezek 18:23). And God's word makes plain that he does not wish any to perish but that all reach repentance (2 Pet 3:9b).

And yet Christ had to mourn, "O Jerusalem, Jerusalem, the city that kills the prophets and stones those who are sent to it! How often would I have gathered your children together as a hen gathers her brood under her wings, and you were not willing!" (Matt 23:37).

Some people take pride in being stubborn, but there is a time to let stubbornness go. Unfortunately, sometimes people decide that it is better to hold on to the presumption of righteousness, blaring out to the universe that they want it done "My Way," as Sinatra's song put it. For some people, this is better than grabbing hold of what is already theirs in Jesus, even as God does not force anyone to grab hold.

And here some people will complain, "But if we can't choose God on our own, then why am I to blame for not trusting in Christ?" Someone needs to say here, "Stop already!"

When God teaches us that we cannot save ourselves or come to him on our own, it is for one purpose. That purpose is not to tell us that we are condemned to be cast into hell, but it is for the one purpose of humbling us, that we would renounce our pride and call on Christ. That phenomenal section in Revelation about the glory of heaven is capped off with this:

> The Spirit and the Bride say, "Come." And let the one who hears say, "Come." And let the one who is thirsty come; let the one who desires take the water of life without price. (Rev 22:17)

But if someone continues to reject Christ, then God has not chosen hell for that person, but the person has chosen it for themselves. So, what is hell? It is indeed what some at the time of the judgment on the last day prefer over God. It is a place that represents a greater commitment to another "god" or "gods," other things that the person preferred to live for. And there is no sufficient way to describe its terrible and horrific reality.

Even for me to write this and for someone else to read it is not for some deranged sense of religion, piety, or legalism, but it is to so alarm us—even those who already have faith in Christ—that we would desperately desire to escape the possibility. God reveals this place so that we would run from it and run towards Christ, and then experience Christ's 100 percent acceptance and love for the sinners who come to him. No strings attached. In the meantime, we cannot claim that the word does not warn about the kind of place hell is.

Holy Scripture calls it the place "where their worm does not die and the fire is not quenched" (Mark 9:47-48). It is the place of a person being bound and cast into "outer darkness" where "there will be weeping and gnashing of teeth" (Matt 22:13). It is an "eternal fire" (Matt 25:41).

CHRIST NEVER DENIES HIS JUSTICE AND MERCY

Christ's mercy for all people is so beyond limitation that he gave his life while we were still his enemies (Rom 5:10). That is to say, Jesus lived, died and rose even for anyone that might eventually go to hell. Even they, he desired to save. Even they, he loved.

Still, there remains for some an insatiable desire to reject the love of God. So, God gives these what they want, and in this way, not only do we see God's mercy but also his justice.

First, we see God's mercy because his mercy which is known through the atonement/covering provided by Christ (through his blood shed to cover sin) is laid out before the sinner. God says in effect, "Here, it is yours.

This is for you. This is to cover *your* sin." So, God's mercy for anyone who chooses hell is given to them free of charge. But then that person throws it aside, rejects it, and effectively says to God, "No, thank you."

Second, we then see God's justice. If one rejects the way God provided for his justice against sin to be satisfied through his Son, then that same justice is claimed upon oneself apart from Christ. Uncovered sin must still be dealt with justly.

Everyone knows this through natural knowledge. Christian or not, if someone commits an egregious offence against another, a judge in a court of law would be scoffed at for giving the offender only a slap on the wrist while avoiding true justice. And yet, people want God to throw away justice at the judgment *even after rejecting the way God dealt mercifully with them so that they could avoid being judged apart from Christ.*

Therefore, God will give people who are condemned what they want. Israel in the Old Testament is an example of this dynamic. When Israel was in the wilderness during the forty years under the leadership of Moses, they complained to Moses and Aaron (and in effect complained against God):

> And the people of Israel said to [Moses and Aaron], "Would that we had died by the hand of the Lord in the land of Egypt, when we sat by the meat pots and ate bread to the full, for you have brought us out into this wilderness to kill this whole assembly with hunger." (Exod 16:3)

But this was not the only time Israel sinned. The wilderness wanderings are filled with accounts of their rebellion against God, even to the extent of committing blatant idolatry (Exod 32). But on this occasion when they had become so enveloped in desiring some *thing* over God, God judged them *by giving them what they wanted* in a way that might teach them to learn about the destructive nature of replacing God with anything.

> And [God said to Moses to] say to the people, "Consecrate yourselves for tomorrow, and you shall eat meat, for you have wept in the hearing of the Lord, saying, 'Who will give us meat to eat? For it was better for us in Egypt.' Therefore the Lord will give you meat, and you shall eat. You shall not eat just one day, or two days, or five days, or ten days, or twenty days, but a whole month, until it comes out at your nostrils and becomes loathsome to you, because you have rejected the Lord who is among you and have wept before him saying, 'Why did we come out of Egypt?'" (Num 11:18–20)

C. S. Lewis describes that moment in a way only he could: "There are only two kinds of people in the end: those who say to God, 'Thy will be done,' and those to whom God says, in the end, 'Thy will be done.'"[6]

GOD'S GRACE AND LOVE FOR SINNERS UNFATHOMABLE

One of my grandkids has been in the toddler stage that includes the extraordinarily cute dialogue with him asking an initial question, and then the adult that falls into his trap by answering his question. This then is met with a new question—namely, "Why?" The moment that "why" question is answered, he then follows that answer with another most sincere and inquiring new "Why?" And so, the chain ensues into an infinite number of "whys."

Similarly, many adults are primed and ready—even after all we have covered—with their ongoing "What about?" questions. What about a person who suffers lifelong addiction? What about a person who is psychotic? What about the person who never had a chance to hear?

The first answer for the "what abouts" is, "Please check your motives for asking." If one asks sincerely, that is one thing, but if one asks as a way out, a delay tactic, or a false plea of agnosticism, then the questions are just rejections of God's love in Christ. You might recall that I referred to the possibility of bad questions above. Well, sometimes, questions might be dangerous even if they are sensical. Sometimes those questions feign sincere seeking and try to hide a hard heart. If that is the case, then it is not time for us to continue asking questions, but it is rather time to confess our sin and call on God's love and mercy in Jesus Christ, the God who took on our flesh and who is the God who is there.

This is the Christ we contend for: the One who desires all to be saved (1 Tim 2:4), that this is no mere hypothesis, but rather a truth that is known, seen, and experienced by real people in real time in the real world.

CHAPTER 11 DISCUSSION GUIDE: CONTENDING FOR THE LIFE EVERLASTING

UNCOVER INFORMATION

1. If God is despised, what of his gifts, including heaven?

6. Lewis, *Great Divorce*, 75.

2. According to Jesus, if one does not know the Scriptures neither can one know what?
3. What should the Christian's attitude be in respect to heaven?
4. Where do the two words "free will" appear in Holy Scripture side by side?
5. According to Jesus in John 15:16, who chooses whom?

DISCOVER MEANING

1. What does it mean for a Christian to have "royal freedom"?
2. How did Saint Augustine qualify "free will"?
3. What is the stance of natural religion or the presumption of righteousness about human ability toward God?
4. How do Christians before physical death start to experience the anticipation of heaven's perfect freedom?
5. How would God have the reality of hell affect people?

EXPLORE IMPLICATIONS

1. If Christ is rejected, how might the idea of heaven be mocked?
2. What is the practical implication of being held captive to the god of this world?
3. If the condition of a person is against God, then what is the condition of their will?
4. If people think themselves to be good, how will this impact their perception about God?
5. What will the bodies of God's people be like as they will be in the glory of Christ, being like him?

Conclusion

Contending for the faith once delivered is the work of the Holy Spirit in and through the baptized, now united to the life, death, and resurrection of Jesus. Giving answer for the saving objective hope and truth that comes from Christ is something our world needs now more than ever before. Will those who claim Jesus do it or avoid it? We know what the sinful flesh would have every Christian do: find the myriad reasons under the sun not to bother contending. The excuses are legion:

1. Only God can do that.
2. I don't want to offend.
3. I shouldn't push my faith onto anyone.
4. People don't need reasonable answers but only to hear that "Jesus loves them."
5. What if I don't know how to answer a question?
6. I don't want to come off as a fanatic.
7. You can't force someone to believe.

Godly contending, however, meets the excuses not to contend head on:

1. God does indeed contend in and through his people who trust him and speaks through them as they rely upon the word of Christ.
2. If Jesus does not offend us, then how can he awaken us from our sin which deceives?
3. There is no pushing allowed nor contentiousness. Only investment in people through the love of Christ.

Conclusion

4. People need everything that God says they need. Jude 3 (as well as 1 Pet 3:15 and other Scriptures) include apologetics in the enterprise of the Great Commission.

5. If we do not know the answer, then God is providing opportunity both for humility and integrity: humility to say, "I don't know," and integrity to say, "But I will find out."

6. Those who contend are not fanatics but join the ranks of those who genuinely love their neighbor. If serving the neighbor through contending for the faith is fanatical, then that is what true love must be while the rest of the world's "love" grows cold.

7. Contending has nothing to do with forcing but has everything to do with reliance upon the Holy Spirit and trusting Jesus.

Many without Christ wonder if Christians really care. They might hold the view that Christians *claim* to know God, but what is often witnessed in their actions does not coincide with contending for the faith which invests in people, but rather a contentiousness which demonizes. It is easy for many to wonder if Christians today desire to hate more than they desire to love.

Contending says, loud and clear, "I care about what you think because God cares about what you think." Contending for the faith says, "Your questions are important to me because they are important to God." Contending says, "Allow me to share with you one of the most powerful statements of faith that gives overflowing hope in this world—the Apostles' Creed—and let me demonstrate what this faith leads to: Christians who contend and therefore Christians who care, really care, for their neighbors."

Bibliography

Anderson, Ryan T. *When Harry Became Sally: Responding to the Transgender Moment.* New York: Encounter, 2019.

Augustine. *The Enchiridion.* In *Doctrinal Treatises*, 229–76. Vol. 3 of *The Nicene and Post-Nicene Fathers*, Series 1. Edited by Philip Schaff. 14 vols. Peabody, MA: Hendrickson, 1995.

———. *On Grace and Free Will.* In *Anti-Pelagian Writings*, 436–65. Vol. 5 of *The Nicene and Post-Nicene Fathers*, Series 1. Edited by Philip Schaff. 14 vols. Peabody, MA: Hendrickson, 1995.

———. *On Rebuke and Grace.* In *Anti-Pelagian Writings*, 468–91. Vol. 5 of *The Nicene and Post-Nicene Fathers*, Series 1. Edited by Philip Schaff. 14 vols. Peabody, MA: Hendrickson, 1995.

Bauer, Walter, et al. *Greek-English Lexicon of the New Testament and Other Early Christian Literature.* 2nd ed. Chicago: University of Chicago Press, 1979.

Bole, Cliff, dir. "The Best of Both Worlds." *Star Trek: The Next Generation*, season 3, episode 26. Aired June 16, 1990.

Bruce, F. F. *The Defense of the Gospel in the New Testament.* Grand Rapids: Intervarsity, 1977.

———. *The New Testament Documents: Are They Reliable?* Grand Rapids: Eerdmans, 1981.

Copan, Paul. "A Moral Argument." In *To Everyone an Answer: A Case for the Christian Worldview*, edited by Francis J. Beckwith et al., 108–23. Downers Grove, IL: InterVarsity, 2004.

Dawkins, Richard. *The God Delusion.* London: Transworld, 2006.

Edwards, Mark J., ed. *Galatians, Ephesians, Philippians.* Ancient Christian Commentary on Scripture: New Testament 8. Downers Grove, IL: Intervarsity, 1999.

Espinosa, Alfonso. "The Apocalyptic Anxiety of American Evangelicalism as Seen Through Left Behind and Tim LaHaye's Programme for the Preservation of Evangelical Identity." PhD diss., University of Birmingham, UK, 2009.

———. "Apologetics as Pastoral Theology." In *Theologia et Apologia: Essays in Reformation Theology and Its Defense Presented to Rod Rosenbladt*, edited by Adam S. Francisco et al., 317–29. Eugene, OR: Wipf & Stock, 2007.

———. "Creation." In *The Lutheran Difference*, edited by Edward A. Engelbrecht et al, 1–64. St. Louis: Concordia, 2007.

———. *Faith That Engages the Culture.* St. Louis: Concordia, 2021.

———. *Faith That Sees Through the Culture.* St. Louis: Concordia, 2018.

———. *Faith That Shines in the Culture.* St. Louis: Concordia, 2023.

Bibliography

Geivett, R. Douglas. "The *Kalam* Cosmological Argument." In *To Everyone an Answer: A Case for the Christian Worldview*, edited by Francis J. Beckwith et al., 61–76. Downers Grove, IL: InterVarsity, 2004.

Gregory of Nazianzus. *Select Letters of Gregory Nazianzen*. Vol. 7 of *The Nicene and Post-Nicene Fathers*, Series 2. Edited by Philip Schaff. Peabody, MA: Hendrickson, 1995.

Habermas, Gary R. *The Historical Jesus: Ancient Evidence for the Life of Christ*. Joplin, MO: College Press, 1996.

———. "The Historical Jesus and the Resurrection." Defending the Faith Lectures, Series 2, Biola University, La Mirada, CA, Fall, 1999.

Habermas, Gary R., and Michael R. Licona. *The Case for the Resurrection of Jesus*. Grand Rapids: Kregel, 2004.

Hume, David. *Dialogues Concerning Natural Religion*. New York: Penguin, 1990.

Just, Arthur A., Jr. *Luke 1:1—9:50*. St. Louis: Concordia, 1996.

Kleinig, John W. *Hebrews*. St. Louis: Concordia, 2017.

LaHaye, Tim, and Thomas Ice. *Charting the End Times*. Eugene, OR: Harvest, 2001.

Lewis, C. S. *The Great Divorce*. New York: HarperCollins, 1946.

Luther, Martin. *Career of the Reformer III*. Edited by Philip S. Watson et al. Luther's Works 33, American ed. Philadelphia: Fortress, 1972.

———. *The Christian in Society II*. Edited by Walther I. Brandt. Luther's Works 45, American ed. Philadelphia: Fortress, 1962.

———. *Church and Ministry III*. Edited by Eric W. Gritsch et al. Luther's Works 41, American ed. Philadelphia: Fortress, 1966.

———. *Lectures on Deuteronomy*. Edited by Jaroslav Pelikan et al. Luther's Works 9, American ed. St. Louis: Concordia, 1960.

———. *Lectures on Galatians 1535: Chapters 1–4*. Edited by Jaroslav Pelikan et al. Luther's Works 26, American ed. St. Louis: Concordia, 1963.

———. *Lectures on Genesis: Chapters 38–44*. Edited by Jaroslav Pelikan et al. Luther's Works 7, American ed. St. Louis: Concordia, 1965.

———. *Lectures on Titus, Philemon, and Hebrews*. Edited by Jaroslav Pelikan et al. Luther's Works 29, American ed. St. Louis: Concordia, 1968.

———. *Luther's Small Catechism with Explanation*. St. Louis: Concordia, 2017.

———. *Selected Psalms III*. Edited by Jaroslav Pelikan. Luther's Works 14, American ed. St. Louis: Concordia, 1958.

———. *Word and Sacrament I*. Edited by E. Theodore Bachmann. Luther's Works 35, American ed. Philadelphia: Fortress, 1960.

Manske, Charles L., and Daniel N. Harmelink. *World Religions Today: Comparative Outlines of Contemporary Faiths Around the World*. Irvine, CA: Institute of World Religions, 1996.

McCain, Paul Timothy, et al., eds. *Concordia: The Lutheran Confessions; A Reader's Edition of the Book of Concord*. 2nd ed. St. Louis: Concordia, 2006.

McGerr, Patricia. "Johnny Lingo and the Eight-Cow Wife." *Australian Women's Weekly* 33.41 (1966) 25, 47–48. https://archive.org/details/The_Australian_Womens_Weekly_09_03_1966/mode/2up.

McGrath, Alister E. *A Fine-Tuned Universe: The Quest for God in Science and Theology*. Louisville: Westminster John Knox, 2009.

Meyer, Stephen C. "What Is the Evidence for Intelligent Design and What Are Its Theological Implications?" In *The Comprehensive Guide to Science and Faith*, edited by William A. Dembski et al., 143–50. Eugene, OR: Harvest, 2021.

BIBLIOGRAPHY

Montgomery, John Warwick. *History, Law and Christianity.* Irvine, CA: New Reformation Publications, 2002.

———. "The Quest for Absolutes: Historical Perspectives." Lecture notes from lecture presented at Christ College Irvine, Irvine, CA, 1984–1986.

Moreland, J. P. *Scaling the Secular City: A Defense of Christianity.* Grand Rapids: Baker Academic, 1987.

Paul, Pamela. "As Kids, They Thought They Were Trans. They No Longer Do." *New York Times*, Feb. 2, 2024. https://www.nytimes.com/2024/02/02/opinion/transgender-children-gender-dysphoria.html.

Pelikan, Jaroslav. *The Emergence of the Catholic Tradition (100–600).* Vol. 1 of *The Christian Tradition: A History of the Development of Doctrine.* Chicago: University of Chicago Press, 1971.

Prophet, Elizabeth Clare. *Reincarnation: The Missing Link in Christianity.* With a foreword by Erin L. Prophet. Gardiner, MT: Summit University Press, 1997.

Purtill, Richard. "Defining Miracles." In *In Defense of Miracles: A Comprehensive Case for God's Action in History*, edited by R. Douglas Geivett et al., 61–72. Downers Grove, IL: InterVarsity, 1997.

Reagan, Ronald. "Remarks at the Annual National Prayer Breakfast." Transcript of speech, Feb. 4, 1988. Ronald Reagan Presidential Library and Museum. https://www.reaganlibrary.gov/archives/speech/remarks-annual-national-prayer-breakfast-6.

Reese, William L. *Dictionary of Philosophy and Religion.* Amherst, NY: Humanity Books, 1999.

Rhodes, Ron. *The 10 Things You Need To Know About Islam.* Eugene, OR: Harvest House, 2007.

Ross, Hugh. *The Creator and the Cosmos.* Covina, CA: Reasons to Believe, 2018.

Schaff, Philip, ed. *The History of Creeds.* Vol. 1 of *The Creeds of Christendom: With a History and Critical Notes.* Revised by David S. Schaff. Grand Rapids: Baker, 1998.

Siemon-Netto, Uwe. "Where Muslim Dreams May Lead." *Quadrant* 60 (2016) 38–41.

Strobel, Lee. *The Case for Faith: A Journalist Investigates the Toughest Objections to Christianity.* Grand Rapids: HarperCollins, 2000.

Tertullian. *Apology.* In *Latin Christianity: Its Founder, Tertullian*, 17–55. Vol. 3 of *The Ante-Nicene Fathers.* Edited by Alexander Roberts and James Donaldson. 10 vols. Peabody, MA: Hendrickson, 1995.

Wachowski, Lana, and Lilly Wachowski, dirs. *The Matrix.* Burbank, CA: Warner Bros. Pictures, 1999.

Topical & Names Index

A priori, 120
Abandonment, 45
Abortion on demand, 162
Actual sins, 23
Addiction, 33
Agape, 150
AI, 10, 22, 34, 62, 63
Alcohol, 113
Ambrose, 146
Another law, 50
Anthropic principle, 59
Apocalyptic genre, 129
Apologetics, xiii, xiv
Apostles' Creed, xiv, 11, 12, 13, 14, 19,
　　20, 27, 39, 57, 58, 88
Apostolic Fathers, 81
Archaeology, 83
Arius, 70, 155
Atonement, 175
Audible word, 145
Augustine, 22, 28, 55, 170, 171

Bean, 169
Bear in a trap, 47, 48
"Bell," 30, 31
Beloved Children, 39
Bibliographical evidence, 80, 81, 82
Binding of sins, 148
Biotechnology, 10, 34, 63
Blessed Hope, 129
Bloom, John, 48
Bodies as canvasses, 34
Body and spirit, 156
Book of Concord, 90
Borg, 31, 153, 154

Bottom-up approach, 115
Bridegroom, 39
Bruce, F.F., 75, 81, 82, 83, 84
Buddhism, 96, 113
Bush, 24, 34, 35

Callings, 150
Chaotic state, 33
Charam/Devote to destruction, 104,
　　105, 106
Category mistake, 55, 56, 162
Cerinthus, 155
Christ as bridegroom, 38, 39
Christ as priest, 100, 101, 115
Christ emptied Himself, 90, 91, 92
Christ's divine nature, 70, 71, 90
Christ's human nature, 70, 71, 90, 108
Church, 141, 142, 143, 144, 145, 146,
　　147, 148, 149, 150
Church militant, 142
Civil unrest, 33
Clipping, 24
Closed universe, 72, 73
Communication, 6, 7, 8, 9, 10, 11
Communion of saints, 13
Compassion, 38
Compatibilism, 25
Compound the "off-ness," 37
Confession and absolution, 26
Conscience, 49, 50
Contend, 1, 2, 3, 4, 5, 6
Contending Christian, 32, 33
Copan, Paul, 61, 62
Core sin, 23
Cosmetics, 34

Topical & Names Index

Craig, William Lane, xvi, 56
Creation, 52, 54, 55, 73, 131
Cross, 100, 109, 128, 150
Crosses, 128, 142, 150
Culture, 10, 11, 13, 14, 30, 31, 32, 33, 34, 35, 37

Darby, John Nelson, 132, 133
Davies, Paul, 59
Dawkins, Richard, 41
Death of death, 113, 121
Descended into hell, 12
Delusional, 7
Demonic, 32, 33, 105, 109, 111
Demonized, 5
Devil, 31, 32, 134, 143
Devil's devil, 112, 113
Determinism, 25
Detransitioned, 37
Dialegomai/To argue, 9
Direct and personal absolution, 147
Disease, 43, 109, 110, 165, 173
Disneyland, 169
Dispensationalism, 132, 133, 135
Dissociating, 37
DNA, 58
Docetism, 155
Dysphoria's, 39

Early, 118
Eastern religious motifs, 19
Eight cows, 38
Einstein, 132
Elijah, 158, 159
Empathy, 38
Empty tomb, 121
Epicurus, 43, 45
Essential "I," 27, 38, 150
Estates, 37, 45, 150
Eternal progression, 155
Evil, 43, 44, 45, 48, 105, 171
Experiential phenomena, 164
Extreme poverty, 33
Eyes of Jesus, 38
Eye-witness testimony, 76, 82, 118

False gods, 39

Falsifiability, 78, 79
Families, 39, 45
Family estate, 45
Fathers, 39, 45
Father's Reputation, 45
Fearmongering, 132, 134
Fides quae, 3
Fides qua, 3
Firstfruits, 165
First parents, 21, 22, 25, 94
Flew, Anthony, 73
Foreknowledge, 25
Foretelling, 84, 85
Forgiveness includes restoration and healing, 150, 156
Formal freedom, 170
Forthtelling, 84, 85
Free will, 168, 170, 171
Fruitful labor, 130

Gamaliel, 126, 127
Gender dysphoria, 36, 37
Gentiles, 49
Gnosticism, 156
God
    as shepherd, 103
    died, 89
    delusion, 41
    obliges, 42
    the Father, 46, 47, 55, 64
    who can be known, 39
God's body, 35
God's justice, 176
Goldilocks effect, 62
Good News of Jesus Christ, 71
Gospel/Good News, xiii, xiv, 4, 7, 32, 38, 46, 93, 153
Great tribulation, 129
Greatest commandment, 97
Greek mythology, 52
Gregory of Nyssa, 89
Guarantee to the believer, 146
Guilt, 21, 148, 153, 154

Habermas, Gary R., 80, 117, 118, 119
Harrison, Edward, 60
Heartbreak, 43

Topical & Names Index

Heaven, 161, 162, 163, 167, 168, 171, 172, 173, 174
Heavenly Father, 39, 45, 47, 52, 61
Hell, 12, 47, 113, 162, 163, 174, 175, 176, 177
Herod, 75, 109, 125
Holy Baptism, 4, 27, 145, 146, 149, 159
Holy Bible, 11, 20, 74, 76, 77, 78, 79, 83, 97, 102, 114
Holy Spirit, xiii, xiv, 2, 3, 4, 21, 35, 44, 46, 85, 99, 112, 115, 132, 142, 143, 144, 145, 148, 149, 163
Holy Trinity, 11, 69, 132
Hormone therapy, 36
Hoyle, Fred, 59
Human nature, 30
Human reason, 54, 160
Hume, David, 43, 73
Humiliation of Christ, 90
Husband, 35, 145, 146
Hyper-individualism, 34
Hypocrisy, 5, 77

I AM, 116
Identifiable marks, 142
Imago Dei, 21
"In Christ," 5, 13, 27, 78, 92, 114, 128, 142, 161, 162, 165, 170, 173
Incarnation, 69, 70, 71, 155
Inclusive *and* exclusive, 93
Ineptitude, 43
Inner conflict, 26
Internal evidence, 80, 82
Inward tendency, 63
Islam, 96, 97

Jasa, Mark, 153
Jenkins, Jerry, 133
Jesus, xiii, 1, 6, 7, 8, 12, 13, 32, 38, 46, 47, 64, 69, 70, 71, 78, 79, 80, 82, 83, 84, 85, 88, 89, 90, 91, 92, 93, 95, 97, 98, 99, 100, 101, 103, 106, 108, 109, 110, 111, 112, 114, 115, 116, 117, 118, 119, 120, 121, 124, 125, 126, 127, 128, 129, 130, 133, 134, 135, 141, 150, 155, 156, 157, 159, 160, 161, 163, 165, 167, 170, 175, 177, 179, 180
Joachim de Fiora, 132
John the Baptist, 85, 111, 126, 158, 159
Johnny Lingo, 38
Josephus, 75, 83
Just, Arthur, 75, 76

Kalam cosmological argument, 56
Karma, 95, 96, 154, 155, 161, 163
Kreeft, Peter, 47
Kenyon, Sir Frederic G., 81
Keys, 147, 148, 149
Kleinig, John W., 100, 101, 102

LaHaye, Tim, 133
Last Day, 129, 134, 135
Law of non-contradiction, 93, 157
Laws of nature, 72, 73
Left Behind, 133, 134
Legalism, 38, 175
Lewis, C.S., 177
Licona, Michael R., 117, 118
Life, 45, 52, 53, 59, 62, 77, 93, 100, 111, 112, 113, 114, 127, 129, 130, 150, 161, 162, 165, 168, 171, 172
Lindsey, Hal, 133
Living incarnationally, 10
Lord's Prayer, 11
Luther, ix, x, xi, 2, 3, 27, 57, 58, 70, 89, 95, 103, 104, 112, 113, 142, 143, 144, 145, 170

Male and Female, 21, 36, 37, 63
Marx, 21
Mass hallucinations, 117
Matrix, 19, 23
McGerr, Patricia, 38
McGrath, Alister, 54, 55
Mere knowledge, 50
Meyer, Stephen C., 58, 59
Micah, 158
Miracle, 71, 72, 73, 85
Money, 32, 43
Monotheism, 46
Montgomery, John Warwick, xvi, 80, 81, 118, 120

Topical & Names Index

Moral Absolutes, 34
Moralism, 38
Moreland, J.P., xvi, 55, 56, 57
Most wonderous love, 46
Mystical communion, 142

Natural knowledge of God, 20, 49, 50, 95, 135, 176
Natural religion, 14, 93, 94, 95, 96, 97, 98, 99, 154, 161, 162, 163, 171
Natural revelation, 20, 49, 50, 53, 95
Natural tendency, 62
Naturalism/Naturalistic view, 61, 62, 72, 73
Negative threats, 32, 33
Neo-Darwinism, 61
Nero, 84
New York Times, 35
Newman, John Henry, 54, 55
Nicodemus, 7
Nightmare come to life, 44
No room for legend or myth, 119
non posse non peccare (not able not to sin), 22
non posse peccare (unable to sin), 22
non sequiturs, 142
"not-right," 20, 23

Obsession, 33
Objective moral values, 61, 62
Off-ness, 14, 26, 34, 37, 38, 49, 50, 63, 135
Office of Christ in the flesh, 148
Omniscience, 25, 105
One-shot at eternity, 161, 162
Ongoing feast, 147
Only Begotten, 46
Open universe, 72, 73
Original sin, 23
Outward tendency, 63

Paley, William, 54, 60
Pascal, Blaise, 53
Passover plot, 120, 121
Paul, Pamela, 35
Pavlov's dogs, 30
Pelikan, Jaroslav, 13
Personal autonomy, 10

Peter, St., 7, 9, 77, 78, 91, 117, 126, 127, 131, 132, 148, 159, 173, 174
Plastic surgery, 34
Political activism, 135
Pontius Pilate, 12, 13, 79, 80, 84, 120
Portal, 33
Posse peccare, posse non peccare (able to sin, able not to sin), 22
Present-day wrath, 49
Presumption of righteousness, 95, 162, 163, 170, 171, 174
Prevention, 39
Pride, 32, 94, 163, 174, 175
Problem of Evil, 43
Prophet, Elizabeth Clare, 154, 160, 161
Prophet, Erin, 161
Prophecy, 84, 85, 134, 158
"Proving" God's existence, 9, 54, 55, 115
Purpose of the Law, 97
Purtill, Richard, 72, 73

Quirinius, 74, 75, 76

Racism, 33
Rapture, 134, 135
Real human history, 74, 84
Reincarnation, 70, 154, 156, 157, 158, 159, 160, 161, 162
Relativism, xiii, 34
Remembering past lives, 163
Removal of Prayer, 33
Resonance, 54, 56, 115
Restoration of our minds, 173
Resurrection counters reincarnation, 156
Resurrection of Jesus Christ, 79, 108, 115, 117, 118
Rhodes, Ron, xvi, 76, 82, 96
Rich man and Lazarus, 47
Robertson, A.T., 81
Roman centurion, 110
Rose again from the dead, 12, 13, 108
Ross, Hugh, 59, 60

Sacrament of continuation, 146
Sacrament of initiation, 146
Sacraments, 3, 99, 134, 149, 159
Sacred writings, 144

Topical & Names Index

Sacrificial Love, 46
Saints, 13
Sarita, 38
Satan, 30, 31, 32, 33, 77, 89, 94, 114, 134, 154, 163, 164
Satan's activity, 42, 163
Satan's chapel, 143, 144
Schaff, Philip, x, 11
Scofield, C.I., 133
Scriptura Scripturam Interpretatur, 158
Seal, 145, 146, 149
Second coming of Christ, 130, 132, 134
Self-isolation, 63
Sex, 32, 36
Sexual Revolution, 33
Shaeffer, Francis, 49
Shame, 21, 38, 148, 153, 154
Shapeshifting, 31, 32, 153, 154
"Sheriff's in town" effect, 48
Skepticism, 34, 42, 71
Social construct, 61
Son of God, 27, 32, 46, 92, 99, 101, 127
Son of Man, 115, 125, 126
Spiritual Battle, 33, 168
Stages, 22, 26, 30
Stage two, 23, 25, 26, 27, 30, 35, 63, 128, 170
Stage three, 26, 27, 28, 35, 114, 128, 142, 150
Star Trek, 31, 153
Stephen, St., 58, 128
Strong delusion, 42, 163
Substitutional descriptions, 92
Swoon theory, 120
Sympathy, 38, 48, 101, 102
Syrophoenician woman, 110

Tacitus, 80, 83, 84
Tattoos, 34
Temple, 3, 8, 35, 46, 92, 112, 116, 125, 127, 129, 133, 143, 155
Ten Commandments, 97
Test of orthodoxy, 85

Test of truth, 85
The God Who Is There, 42, 49, 54, 100, 101, 104, 105, 109, 111, 114, 115, 131, 142, 149, 150, 163, 164, 165, 168, 177
Theism, 57, 73
Thomas, 117, 156, 157
Those who suppress the truth, 49
Time, 11, 13, 55, 56, 69, 74, 75, 80, 85, 117, 118, 119, 131, 132, 134, 146, 155, 157, 161, 162, 173, 177
Transfiguration, 77, 159, 173
Transitioning, 36
Transmigration of the soul, 114, 154, 161
Transsexuality, 34
Two "I's," 27, 28

Unflattering stories, 76
Universal plight, 22
Universe, xi, 6, 41, 54, 55, 56, 57, 58, 59, 60, 61, 62, 72, 73, 109, 116, 135

Vicariously, 71
Vicious cycle, 24
Victoria's Secret model, 37

Wager (Pascal's), 53
Weakness of God, 93
What am I? 26, 35
Where are You?! 43
Where do we find God? 47
Where is God? 41, 121, 148, 149
Who am I? 35
Wilderness temptation, 32
World, 142, 146, 150
World Wars, 33
Word of God, 3, 4, 6, 20, 27, 32, 37, 79, 83, 102, 109, 143, 144, 148, 154, 159
Wrecked bodies will become glorious, 173
Wrestling with big brother, 91

Scriptural Index

Genesis
1:3	6, 102
1:27	21
1:31	155, 172
2:7	109
3:15	89, 134
5, 10 & 11	76
6:5	22
11	62
13:10	76
32	103
32:6	103

Exodus
3:14	116
7:11	164
7:12	164
7–12	164
16:3	176
32	176
33:11	159

Numbers
11:18–20	176
21	104

Deuteronomy
1:1–2	76
2	104
3	104
18	159
18:9–12	164
18:15	159
31:6	46

Joshua
6	104
11	104

1 Samuel
2:30	148

1 Kings
19:11	6
19:12	6
24:5	76

2 Kings
2:11	159
2:11–12	158

1 Chronicles
1–9	76
28:20	46

Job
2:9	132
2:10	44, 51

Psalms

8:3-4	42
16:11	168
19:1	60
23	103
23:1	103
39:4-5	131
103:12	102
105	76
119:105	27

Proverbs

14:12	165
16:18	94
28:14	42
31:6-7	113
31:8	162

Ecclesiastes

1:9	10
3:11	135

Isaiah

7:14	112
25:6	174
40:1-2	6
43:25	102
53	103
53:5	92
53:6	103
53:7b	8
53:12b	103

Jeremiah

15:16	144
31:34b	102

Lamentations

3:22-23	102

Ezekiel

18:23	174
33:11	49

Micah

4:5	158
7:18-19	103

Malachi

3:6	4

Matthew

1	76, 105
3:9	111
5:12a	167
5:44-45	3
6:21-22 & 27-28	98
8:5-13	110
8:11	174
9:10-13	110
11:11-14	158
11:28	7
14:30	77
15:10, 18-19	98
15:16	77
15:21-28	110
16:11	77
16:15	126
16:16	126
16:17	127
16:18	4, 127
16:19	147
16:21	125
16:21-26	124
16:22	132
16:23	77
16:24	141
17:4	77
17:22-23	124
18:18	147
18:20	127
18:21	148
18:22	148
19:6b	145
20:17-19	125
21:31	163
22:13	175
22:23-30	168
22:37	97
22:37-39	xiii

22:39	97	1:13	158
22:40	97	1:17	158
23:28	163	2:1–5	74
23:37	8, 174	3:1–2	76
24:1–2	125	4:3	32
24:6, 7 & 12	43	4:6	32
25	135	4:9–11	32
25:10	174	5:4–6	7
25:40	38, 150	5:5	77
25:41	175	5:8	7
26:26–28	147	5:20–24	115
26:52–53	92	7:1–10	110
26:69–75	77	7:9–10	110
27:40	92, 112	7:11–17	111
27:42	92	8:40–56	111
27:46	45	8:41	111
28:9	117	9:22–25	124
28:17	117	9:33	77
28:18	134	9:43b–45	124
28:20b	127	10:16	149
		10:18	134
		10:41–42	145, 151
		13:29	174

Mark

7:24–30	110	16:29–31	47
8:31–37	124	18:31–34	125
8:33	77	21:5–6	125
9:5	77	21:27	129
9:30–32	124	21:28	129
9:31	125	22:19–20	147
9:33–34	77	22:24	77
9:47–48	175	22:55–65	77
10:13	77	23:8	109
10:21	8	23:34	8
10:32–34	125	23:43	168
11:15–17	8	24:31	117
13:1–2	125	24:34	117
14:22–24	147	24:36	117
14:62	115		
14:66–72	77		
16:9	117		
16:12	117		
16:14	117		

John

1:1–3	6
1:1 & 14	69, 70, 102
1:21	158
2:13–17	8
2:19 & 21	112, 116
2:20	125
3	7

Luke

1	76
1:2	76
1:1–3	76

John (continued)

3:3–8	20
3:10	7
3:16	7, 45, 51
5:24	26
6:37, 39	170
6:44	170
6:51	93
6:65	170
7:51	7
8:7	8
8:31	143
8:44	8
8:56–59	116
9:1–7	111
9:41	27
10:10	114
11	111
11:33	106
11:35	112
11:40	112
13:8	77
13:27	8
14:6	93
15:16	170, 178
15:20	141
16:33b	130
18:23	8
18:25–27	77
18:36	135
19:11	125
19:30	134
20	120
20:16	117
20:19	117
20:22–23	147
20:24–28	157
20:26	117
21:7	117
21:24	76

Acts

1:6	117
2	102
2:32	76
2:33 & 41	127
5	126
5:27–29	126
5:33	126
5:35–39	126
5:37	75, 76
7:54	128
7:55–56	128
7:59–60	128
9:4	141
9:5	117, 141
17:2–3	9
17:22	9
20:28	89
22:8	117
22:16	4
26:25–26	76

Romans

1	20, 49
1:17	3
1:18	42
1:18–20	49
1:20	58
2	20
2:14–15	49
3:10 11	22
3:20	97
3:23	8
5:10	175
6:1–2a	148
6:3–4	146
6:14	27
7	26
8:11	112
9:5	116
10:17	4
12:15	38
12:21	1

1 Corinthians

1:18	160
1:21	160
2:9	168
3:3	142
5:1	142
6:1–8	142

Scriptural Index

6:12	62
6:19–20	35
7:4	35
9:22b	10
11:17–22	142
11:23–25	147
13:12	173
15	76, 135
15:1–2	119
15:3	119
15:5	117
15:6	76, 117
15:7	117
15:8	117
15:14	78
15:17	78
15:18	78
15:19	78
15:20	165
15:42–44 & 53b	172
15:42–58	168

2 Corinthians

1:21–22	145
5:7	27, 47
5:21	92
11:14	164
12:2	168
12:4	168

Galatians

1:13	76
1:18	76, 119
2:1	76
2:11–14	77
2:20	27, 29
3:13	92
4:4	69
5	26
5:11	160
5:22–23	99
6:2	101

Ephesians

1:1	13
1:4	45
1:4b–10	25
1:13	145
1:20	112
2:1–2a	22
2:10	99, 143, 161
4:5	146
4:30	145
6:12	2, 33, 168

Philippians

1:20	130
1:23	130
1:27	2, 15
1:28	3
1:29–30	3
2:5–8	90

Colossians

1:15–16	155
1:16	116
2:12	146

1 Thessalonians

4:17	134, 135, 136

2 Thessalonians

2:9–12	164
2:10–12	42, 51

1 Timothy

1:12–17	42, 50
2:4	xiv, 42, 121, 177

2 Timothy

2:25	43
2:26	170
3:2–5	43
3:15	144
3:16	144
3:17	144
4:3–4	76

Titus

2:13	129
3:5	4

Hebrews

1:1–2	84
1:2–3	116
2:14–18	100
4:7	165
4:14–16	101
4:15	101
4:15–16	101
7:25	101
10:24–25	149
11:3	109
11:16	171
13:5	127
13:5–6	46
13:20	112

James

2:10	8
4:7	134
4:14	131

1 Peter

1:8	174
1:25	4
3:15	xiii, 1, 9, 15, 180
3:18–20	12
4:8	174
4:14–16	130

2 Peter

1:16	76
3:1b–9	131, 137
3:8	43, 162
3:9	49
3:9b	174

1 John

1:1	76
1:1–3	76
1:8–9	26
2:2	161
2:15–16	40
3:2	173
4:8 & 16	21
4:19	23
5:3	99, 171

Jude

:3	xiii, 1. 4, 14, 33, 84, 180
:4	2
:3–4	2

Revelation

7:14–17	129
14:13	161
19:9	174
21	135
21:1	172
21:3	172
21:4	172
21:11	172
21:12–15	172
21:18	172
21:21	172
21:23	172
21:26	172
21:27	172
22:1	172
22:2	172
22:13	116
22:17	175

www.ingramcontent.com/pod-product-compliance
Lightning Source LLC
Chambersburg PA
CBHW060606230426
43670CB00011B/1993